TO PUNISH
AND PROTECT

Against a System

That Coddles Criminals

JEANINE PIRRO

WITH CATHERINE WHITNEY

A Touchstone Book
Published by Simon & Schuster
New York London Toronto Sydney

The cases described in this book are real.
In some instances, names and identifying details have been
changed to protect the privacy of the victims. Names that have been
changed are marked with an asterisk.

TOUCHSTONE
Rockefeller Center
1230 Avenue of the Americas
New York, NY 10020

First Touchstone Edition 2004
Published by arrangement with St. Martin's Press

TOUCHSTONE and colophon are registered trademarks
of Simon & Schuster, Inc.

For information regarding special discounts for bulk purchases,
please contact Simon & Schuster Special Sales at 1-800-456-6798
or business@simonandschuster.com.

Designed by Fritz Metsch

Manufactured in the United States of America

3   5   7   9   10   8   6   4

The Library of Congress has cataloged the
St. Martin's Press edition as follows:
Pirro, Jeanine.
To punish and protect : a DA's fight against a system that coddles
criminals / Jeanine Pirro with Catherine Whitney.
p. cm.
1. Pirro, Jeanine.   2. Public prosecutors—New York (State)—
Biography.   3. Criminal justice, Administration of—United States.
4. Criminal law—United States—Cases.   I. Whitney, Catherine.
II. Title.
345.73—dc22   2004270224

ISBN-13: 978-0-7432-6568-3
ISBN-10:   0-7432-6568-8

To my mother, Esther Ferris, the woman who taught me the difference between right and wrong, and good and evil, and who continues to be a daily inspiration to me. I can only hope to do and be the same for my daughter, Kiki, and my son, Alex.

Contents

ACKNOWLEDGMENTS

This book is a collaborative effort. It is the result of the involvement of many people who believe, as I do, that crime victims deserve a public voice. I am grateful for their support, and want to give special thanks to those whose contributions have made this book a reality.

Diane Reverand, my editor at St. Martin's Press, believed in this project from the start, and has been a terrific advocate every step of the way. She has shepherded the work with passion and skill. Sherry Suib Cohen introduced me to Diane, and repeatedly nudged me to put into writing those cases that reflect the battle prosecutors across this country wage every day.

My literary agent, Joni Evans, is a great friend and advisor. Her confidence in me and my message, her creativity, and her unfailing book sense are invaluable.

Catherine Whitney, my collaborator, has been a true colleague and dedicated listener. Her capacity to empathize with the pain of countless crime victims is reflected in the feeling that emanates from the page. Catherine and her writing partner, Paul Krafin, have helped to transform my words and ideas into cogent, readable prose that perfectly captures my intent. Their literary agent, Jane Dystel, has provided invaluable assistance during the process.

The devotion of my staff, the assistant district attorneys, and the investigators at the Westchester District Attorney's office is a daily inspiration to me. They are a remarkable and caring team of professionals, who constantly strive to level the field by making criminals accountable. I thank them all for being models of public service.

David Hebert, Executive Assistant District Attorney, is one of those people few of us ever have an opportunity to meet in the course of our lives, let alone befriend. His wisdom, loyalty, and endless determination to get the job done are without equal.

Richard E. Weill, Chief Assistant District Attorney, is both brilliant and generous with his time, always maintaining the highest standards of integrity.

Roseanne Pesce is an invaluable assistant, whom I thank every day for keeping me organized and on schedule. She is smart, resourceful, and she refuses to give up.

My family has my continued gratitude for their love, support, and the daily lessons they teach me about the important things in life. They anchor me and make the work I do possible.

Finally, I want to thank the countless wonderful men, women, and children who have crossed my path over the years—those victims who demonstrated great courage and resolve in the face of enormous odds. They are the heroes who give meaning to those of us who do the work of criminal justice.

Justice is blind; but, fortunately for the sake of the welfare of society, she can often see through the bandage.

—Voltaire

As this edition of *To Punish and Protect* was preparing to go to press, I announced my candidacy for the United States Senate. My mother was in the front row of the audience that day. She has always been my role model and my mentor. Watching her selfless actions on behalf of neighbors in need, and hearing her brave voice raised to defend the just against the unjust, helped formulate my own moral core.

I believe that people deserve to live in communities where they can walk down the streets without fear of assault or harassment; enjoy the fruits of their labor without fear that corporate fraud, identity theft, or street crime will leave them devastated; and raise their children without fear that sexual predators, gang violence, or drugs will steal their innocence and perhaps their lives. I believe that the elderly deserve to live out their golden years without abuse or neglect, and that women deserve to be safe from assault in their own homes. These are pretty basic goals in a civilized society, but my staff of prosecutors and investigators must fight every day to see them realized.

Thirty years in law enforcement have also shown me that the job of protecting the public must extend to every area of their lives. It's not just the protection against crime. Providing security means making sure people have the resources to take care of themselves financially. It means growing our communities and creating long-term job stability. It means making sure people have the health care they need.

As district attorney I have been committed to speaking out for the rights of the victims of crime who have no voice of their own. But I have often found that the criminal devastation that brings them to my office is only one piece of a larger victimization. If we are to be guardians of the public well-being, we must strengthen people's economic and social defenses and decrease their risk of becoming victims in the first place.

Our challenge is to ask the hard questions, beginning with these: Do we as a society have the will and the courage to demand that every citizen be guaranteed a place within the social contract that binds the government to its people? Are we committed to protecting the weak as well as the strong? Can we respond not only to big public emergencies but also to the institutional, long-term needs that take decades to remedy?

While growing up in Elmira, a small town in upstate New York, my parents taught me that individuals can make a difference and that people can fix what's broken. It's a lesson I've never forgotten. Every day for thirty years I've lived that lesson, throwing myself into my work, eager to get my hands dirty and get things done.

I learned to fight in the small arena of Elmira. Today I understand that all communities in New York and across the nation share a common need for someone who will fight on their behalf, for representation that mixes passion with practical action.

Politicians often bury the message in layers of rhetoric. Or they make excuses and list the reasons people do bad things—a futile exercise that abandons the cause of justice. For me, it has always been very simple. It comes down to knowing the difference between right and wrong, and deciding what we're going to do about it. That's my cause and my life's work.

Jeanine Pirro
October 2005

The Battleground

The office of district attorney is a battleground where the fight between good and evil unfolds each day. We see the ugliest side of life, the pain that people go through for no reason. They didn't do anything. They didn't ask for it. Yet here they are living their personal nightmares. We cannot take away their pain or turn back time to undo the damage, but we can be the avengers. We can seek justice on their behalf.

Mine is an elected position, and I am a public servant. In Westchester County, New York, where I serve, that involves protecting the welfare of nearly one million people in a 433-square-mile area. It also involves prosecuting more than 33,000 criminal cases a year. I began my first term as district attorney of Westchester County,

New York, in 1994, and before that I was a county court judge, also an elected position, for three years. We live in a time of great cynicism and mistrust toward elected officials, who are widely viewed as seeking personal power and celebrity at the expense of the citizenry. This book is an effort to rise above the current climate of cynicism and to restore luster to the ideal of public service. I work for the people, and it is their stories that I recall here, the campaigns I have waged on their behalf that have engaged me so completely.

The heroes of this book are the victims and their families. They have persevered through the darkest nights, frequently without much support from the system. Although my office investigates and prosecutes all types of illegal activity—gang violence, narcotics, environmental destruction, organized crime, and others—I have chosen to focus on those crimes whose scars remain after the wounds have healed, those whose victims cry out to us, often from the grave, and demand that we acknowledge them.

This book is not a memoir, although it is extremely personal, since the quest for justice has been a central part of my identity for as long as I can remember. When I was six years old I announced that I was going to be a lawyer and fight for the underdog. The adults all thought that was cute. They said, "That's nice, Jeanine, but don't you want to be a mommy?" In the 1950s it was nearly unfathomable that one could do both. The role models of my early youth were women who had made clear-cut choices between having a family and pursuing a profession. I didn't dream of my wedding day. I dreamed of standing in the well of a courtroom.

When I began working as an assistant district attorney in Westchester County in 1975, women prosecutors were not common. Many people could not accept the idea that a woman could do a "man's" job.

Often, victims and witnesses came to the office and, upon seeing me, demanded to speak with a "real" prosecutor. I have chaired meetings of law enforcement officers where I was asked to serve coffee before stepping up to the podium.

Much has changed in the past thirty years. It is no longer unthinkable for a woman to have both a family and a profession. But I still have to fight to keep the focus on the issues in a way that no man in my position ever has to. When I speak to civic groups or sit for press interviews people are always very curious to know more about me—to explore the details of my personal life and my feelings. That's natural. I'm a woman in what has traditionally been a man's job. I am a wife and mother, a person with emotional commitments beyond my office. But this book is not about my marriage, family, tax returns, or pet pigs, Homer and Wilbur. At various times, all of these have been the subject of intense press interest.

The media has a voyeur's fascination with those aspects of women officials' lives. We learn to live with it, while challenging the public to view us through the force of our ideas and actions, not the length of our skirts or the style of our hair. My ideas and actions involve giving a public voice to victims who cannot speak for themselves. *To Punish and Protect* is about them, not about me.

When I look at the state of our criminal justice system, I don't see many shades of gray. Unlike the legal scholars who dwell in theoretical settings, my world is cut-and-dry, black-and-white. It's simple, really. In my view, it all comes down to knowing the difference between right and wrong. And once we establish that, what's left is deciding what we're going to do about it.

Do we as a society have the will and the courage to pursue justice, to demand that the rights and privileges guaranteed in our Constitution and Bill of Rights embrace every citizen? Today, too many victims of crime remain outside the social contract—removed from the power that would guarantee justice. That's a problem, not only for the individuals who are victimized, but for our communities as well. Every time a victim is ignored, or a criminal goes unpunished, or violence is excused, our society erodes further. It becomes harder, meaner, and more violent. Without redress, victims become despairing and embittered; often they exact their price by victimizing others. And so it goes. We all understand the cycle of violence. Do we have the will and the courage to end it?

In the pages of this book I will tell you stories that I wish could be relegated to the pages of a novel, rather than to the cold reality of nonfiction. No one wants to believe that predators roam freely in our midst, or that brutal acts can be committed in the sanctity of a marriage that was formed in love, or that elderly parents can be beaten and abused by adult children who no longer have any use for them. But the first step to healing the ills of society is to face the truth. Only then can we act together to make our communities safe for ourselves and our children.

CHAPTER 1

Cage the Bastards

My job as a district attorney is to enforce the law. That means I often have to deal with slime. This was the case on an October day in 2002. Barry Johnson* was the very definition of slime. If the law had allowed me to feed this angelic-looking young pedophile to wild animals, I might have been tempted. But that would have been an insult to all the animals I've ever known.

At a conference table in my office, four perfectly nice couples, all good parents, sat stunned, disbelieving. The night before they had learned that their twelve- and thirteen-year-old daughters had been held for some

*Not his real name.

time in the grip of a cunning sexual predator. The details were almost more than they could bear.

Barry Johnson was a twenty-four-year-old youth counselor at a local church. He wasn't your typical creep on the street. Barry was clean-cut, charming, and sincere, with a handsome, friendly face and a mop of tousled blondy curls. The kids in the church group adored him. Especially the girls; they all giggled and blushed when he smiled at them. People regarded Barry as a role model, the kind of young man they'd be proud to have called their own. Everyone loved to have Barry around. Everyone trusted Barry.

Barry, like so many pedophiles, used trust to lure the girls, one after the other, into his dark world. He promised each of them that he would be their guide, that he would gently introduce them to the mysteries of womanhood. He assured them time and again that there was absolutely nothing wrong with what he asked them to do. He would keep them safe. He would be exquisitely caring, a patient lover who promised to preserve their virginity by only engaging in oral and anal sex.

The girls were swept away. Over time, they would do everything Barry asked. They allowed him to photograph them at each stage of their budding sexual relationships. He convinced one girl to set up an Internet chat room, and to invite her friends to go online and talk to him about sex.

Barry's underground network was expanding. Then

one of the girls told her mother, and just like that Barry's façade was shattered.

It was painful to look into the tortured faces around my conference table—the parents of Barry's victims. One distraught father hunched over the table, clenching and unclenching his fists, his eyes red and burning. A mother who couldn't stop crying swiped at the river of tears flowing helplessly down her cheeks. Another father sat there, mouth agape, shaking his head back and forth, as if to dispel the notion that it was true, that this could actually have happened to his daughter. But most of the parents sat still as stone, their faces empty, their eyes vacant with shock and grief.

I was deeply moved by their plight. Just yesterday everything had been going along normally. They were living their lives, confronting the usual mundane crises that all families come up against. And then this thunderbolt came hurtling down from the sky and tore them apart.

My goal was clear. I was going to put Barry Johnson away, and that involved enlisting the cooperation of the girls and their parents. That day in my office I had another vital job to do—to help the victims begin the process of healing.

Not everyone agrees with me on this. Many of my colleagues think prosecutors should concentrate on the crime and let the social workers and psychiatrists pick up the pieces of the shattered families. That attitude infuriates me. The system depends on victims to help us prosecute criminals. We use them, put them through the wringer, and take advantage of their trauma to make our case. We cannot then say, "Thank you very much. Good luck, good-bye," and throw them away. We must provide a support system for victims to help them heal. To ignore this obligation can lead to more crime, especially when the victims don't have a way to address their hurt or rage. Working with victims is an integral part of my job. It is crucial that my office is more than a clearinghouse for crime.

The parents of the girls were too stunned to say much, but I could read the agonized questions in their eyes: *How could I not have known? How could my daughter have let this happen? How could she not have told me? How will we ever be able to recover from this?* I felt their torment because I would have been asking those same questions had our positions been reversed, and had one of my own children been violated. As I so often had to do in these situations, I fought back my own parental fear— the idea that my son or daughter could be harmed. I realized, though, that the empathy I felt as a mother always snapped me back into a fighting mode. My ability to relate to their horror gave me an added determination to get the bastard who had done this.

I knew from experience that the parents would have a much harder time than their daughters putting this behind them. Right now, the girls seemed more embarrassed and chastened than traumatized. They were too young to fully understand the jeopardy they had been in. The parents would have a tougher challenge. Their guilt and anger would keep the wounds open and festering long after their more resilient children had healed and moved on. It was crucial that the parents get past the guilt they were experiencing so they didn't pass it on to their daughters. Or worse, blame the girls for actions that none of them—parents or children—were able to control.

Even as I tried to console them, my words felt inadequate. "I am so sorry that this has happened, but know that your daughters are going to be okay. You have to help them. Your most important priority right now is to concentrate on healing yourselves and your daughters."

They stared at the table, hearing but not really comprehending. "There is only one person to blame here," I said quietly, "Barry Johnson. Your daughters didn't do anything wrong. It's not their fault. And it's not *your* fault. This didn't happen because you're bad parents, or your daughters are bad girls. Bad things can happen to good people. Young girls are curious—that's a normal thing. They want to experience life. And this guy was extremely cunning and manipulative. He was very good at selling himself to them and gaining their trust. Guys like this—they're incredibly devious and shrewd. They're calculating, savvy predators."

And now came the hardest part. "The grand jury is convening in two days. Your daughters will be called to testify. It's a closed, secret proceeding. The defendant will not be present. And we will do everything in our power to make sure that none of these young women are identified in any way, shape, manner, or form."

They were reacting now, the nos already forming on their lips. I leaned in closer. "Listen, I understand how difficult this will be. I am a mother of two teenagers myself, and I would agonize over this decision. But I know from decades of experience that there's a positive aspect to this. Part of the healing process involves your daughters talking about what happened to them. Yes, they were victims, but we can empower them now. Again, we will protect their identities."

"But if he goes to trial? What then?" a mother asked. Her eyes were bloodshot and puffy. She dabbed at her tears.

"He may try to plead guilty to avoid a trial. But I want significant time on him. If I don't think we'll get enough years, I will not cut a deal. Period. He must not be allowed to do this again. We'll go to trial. If that happens, your daughters will have to testify in court, because it's the defendant's constitutional right to confront his accusers. But the media won't report their names. We will protect your daughters from being victimized any further. I promise you that."

These good men and women, drawing on an inner strength they didn't know they had, slowly nodded their heads in agreement. Their daughters would testify.

• • •

There was a time in our history when these families would have decisively settled the matter themselves. Frontier justice was meted out by one's kin. Women and children were dependent on their fathers, husbands, and brothers to protect them. We have rejected vigilante justice in civilized societies. In exchange for our agreement not to take the law into our own hands, the government promises to protect its citizens and to punish criminals. This is the social contract we have forged. When the girls' parents sought no private vengeance against Barry Johnson they lived up to their part of the contract.

By bringing their daughters to testify they expressed their inherent trust that the system would deliver justice. My sworn duty was to see that the system held its part of the bargain, but I knew something they didn't know. The Wild West has been relegated to the past in more ways than one. Justice is no longer swift and sure. It is slow and uncertain. Over the centuries we have turned the criminal justice system into an intricately woven lattice of law and procedure. At times, the system's purpose—to guarantee that victims are avenged by the state—can be lost. Too often, victims are further scarred by the very system that is designed to protect them.

The prosecutor I assigned to the case was a specialist in child sexual abuse from my Special Prosecution Division. I created this division soon after I became district attorney in 1994, because I knew firsthand that certain victims needed particular care and expertise. The division's handpicked prosecutors have the training, temperament, and compassion to handle the most fragile victims and the most delicate issues. The room where the girls would be interviewed was homey and comfortable, a haven inside the cold concrete structure of the courthouse. We could provide a semblance of softness, even in this setting. We could be nurturing. The assistant district attorneys all know that caring for the victims is a priority in this office.

Each of the girls was interviewed separately as the parents waited outside. The prosecutor needed to determine the exact nature of the crimes that had been committed. She also needed to prepare the girls for what they could expect from the grand jury. In the process she wanted to establish a rapport with the victims, a sense of trust that would make them feel less frightened of the process.

Two days later the girls testified before one of the four grand juries we have sitting every day. It is the task of the grand jury, which is made up of ordinary citizens, just like a trial jury, to listen to evidence and to make a determination about whether or not there is sufficient legal evidence and reasonable cause to charge a person with a crime. All felony indictments issued in New York must pass through the grand jury process.

As I told the parents, the grand jury hearing was secret. This proceeding, unlike a trial, could not be public, nor could the identities of the witnesses be made known. Although the girls' parents could not be present, which was difficult for everyone, the girls were terrific.

I was very proud of them. It takes courage to right a wrong.

In addition to the girls' testimony we had also collected a tremendous amount of other evidence against Barry. In particular, we had possession of videos and pictures that were seized when Barry Johnson was arrested. It was a heart-wrenching, sickening experience to watch those videos. These were images that could keep you awake at night: Adult men having sex with children, and forcing them to have sex with other children. Men masturbating onto the naked genitals of babies. I kept thinking of these innocent little children, forever memorialized in some pervert's downloaded file, one that's been sold or traded to a network of pedophiles across the world.

The grand jury voted to charge Barry with multiple counts of Sexual Abuse and Sodomy in the First Degree. The judge set bail at only $20,000. We vigorously pleaded for a higher bail. In our experience, pedophiles like Barry don't just sit at home praying for redemption while awaiting trial. They collect other victims. They are a continuing danger to the community.

Only weeks before Barry's arrest, we caught a convicted pedophile on the Internet trying to set up a date with a fourteen-year-old boy the night before he was sentenced.

In New York State, as in most states, we don't have preventative bail. We can't make an argument that a defendant might commit additional crimes, even when we have good reason to believe this might occur. The way the law stands now, the amount of bail is sufficient if it assures a defendant's return to court. A judge may consider character, reputation, criminal record, family ties, and employment in making that assessment. These factors, though important, don't address the real issue of concern in cases like Barry Johnson's—that is, the likelihood that the defendant will cause further harm while out on bail.

The outmoded bail statute is a gaping hole in the armor of justice, a situation in which the law fails to consider what is best for the majority rather than the individual. The questions we should be asking are clear and relevant: Are we placing our children at further risk? Is the perpetrator likely to repeat his behavior again? In nearly every state, bail criteria fail to consider the potential danger to the community of a defendant out on bail.

An exception is Arizona. In 2002, Arizona became the first state to pass a bail reform act specifically designed to protect the community against sexual predators. The referendum allows judges to deny bail if the evidence is strong and convincing. If bail is granted, defendants are required to wear electronic monitors. This is a small step in the right direction. There are lobbying efforts in nearly every state to institute similar changes.

In New York, however, we weren't allowed to speculate about Barry Johnson's potential for future predatory acts. That's the law. So, within twenty-four hours of the bail hearing he was released into the bright sunshine of freedom. And I couldn't do a thing to stop him. Yet.

If you walk down the hallway outside my office at the Westchester County Courthouse, you'll get a pretty good idea of what law and order has meant here in the 208 years since the first DA rode into town. The portraits of my predecessors line the walls, and they're a pretty stern lot. All men. My official portrait isn't on the wall yet. I'm afraid it might cause some of the old boys to turn over in their graves.

I'm the first woman to be elected district attorney in Westchester County. Before that I was the first woman elected as a county court judge, and before that I was the first woman in the county to try a homicide case. These firsts are significant, not because they happened to me, but because they are steps forward in making our system more inclusive. As long as women were not represented in positions where policy was formed and laws were made, they could not expect the law to treat them fairly.

Women have traditionally been excluded from participation in and protection from the law. Our society is the product of a history that considered women incapable of testifying because they were believed to lack credibility. We are a product of a history that deemed women incapable of being jurors because they lacked common sense. In 1864 the Supreme Court ruled that women should not be allowed to practice law because they were the weaker sex. We may laugh at these archaic notions, but they haven't completely disappeared in modern times.

In law school I was one of a handful of women in a sea of men. More than once I was criticized for "taking a man's place." Women of my generation often find themselves in the position of breaking new ground in male-dominated fields, and it can be difficult and lonely. Sometimes we're held to a higher, or at least a different, standard. I assure you that none of my male predecessors ever received the media attention I have about the style of their hair, the cut of their suits, or their relative attractiveness. That comes with the territory for a woman, and I'm more amused by it than offended.

I do know this: As a woman who has experienced what it is like to be without power, to be trivialized and not taken seriously, I am able to listen to victims with a different ear. I sense their pain and their feelings of powerlessness. I am able to bring this empathy for victims to the job of law enforcement. It makes a difference.

When victims enter my office, they don't encounter an intimidating or impersonal environment. I am a public servant—*their* servant—and I think of my office as their living room. It is warm and inviting, with comfortable couches where we can sit together as equals. One of my desk drawers is filled with toys for those times when children are involved. My coffeepot is always on, and a small refrigerator is stocked with soft drinks. Boxes of tissues are within easy reach, as many tears are shed in my office. These small gestures can make the critical difference, especially when individuals are frightened and reluctant to testify.

The position of district attorney has traditionally been defined in macho terms. You have to be tough on crime. Your goal is to lock 'em up and throw away the key. And though I've thrown away a few keys in my day, my ultimate goal goes beyond catching criminals. I can be as dogged in the pursuit of criminals as any man I've ever known, but anyone can fill the jails. I want to make the victims whole again.

To do that, I need the cooperation of the citizenry, the backing of the courts, and the commitment of the lawmakers. Together we must exercise the will and the courage to make our communities better.

However, over the, years, I've witnessed a growing disconnect between the rhetoric about law and justice and the reality of prosecuting crimes and protecting the public.

Every day I face barriers, not just from criminals, but from the system, which prevent me from doing my job. Many laws have nothing whatsoever to do with making our communities safer, protecting our children, reducing violence, or getting predators off the streets. They are designed to protect defendants, but have little to offer to the victims of crime. I believe this imbalance must be remedied.

Defense lawyers are quick to remind us that we shouldn't treat defendants like criminals because of the presumption of innocence. Here's my response: Why don't we tell the truth about the presumption of innocence? The phrase "innocent until proven guilty" does not mean that those of us who have examined all of the evidence before a trial must stick our heads in the sand and draw no conclusions whatsoever. We don't drag people into court because we assume they are innocent; we indict people because we believe they are guilty.

When the grand jury voted to indict Barry Johnson it didn't assume he was innocent. Its vote meant there was probable cause, based on extremely damning evidence, to assume he was guilty. There was victim testimony, hundreds of photographs, videotapes of Barry performing sexual acts with children. It was all there before our eyes. A legitimate response to viewing such depravity would be, "Don't let this dangerous predator back in the community."

Ask any reasonable person if Barry should have been walking the streets, based on what we knew at that point, and they'd say, "God, no." When I broke the news to the girls and their parents they simply couldn't believe it. Like most law-abiding citizens, they thought the system would work to protect them. To discover otherwise was an astonishing realization to these families.

Although we give defendants every possible benefit, even when we have stacks of evidence against them, we pay little attention to the victims or the potential victims. They're invisible. What about their rights?

I focus a lot of energy on the victims of crime, because they're at the very heart of the justice system. The way we treat our own citizens when they are most vulnerable is disgraceful. If you are the victim of a crime you're fair game, an open book.

Defense lawyers can hire investigators to dig into your past. They can call your employer, interrogate your neighbors, destroy your reputation. This isn't done just because they believe you're hiding something, or to uncover significant factors that might shed light on their client's innocence. No. They do it because they can. They're looking for some vague innuendo they can toss in a jury's lap, some tiny grain of doubt that it didn't happen the way you said it did, that you had other motives, that you had it coming. The quest has little to do with the truth. Even when the defendant admits to his lawyer that he is guilty—that the victim is telling the truth—the defense attorney is still permitted to attack the victim with outrageous suggestions.

Several years ago my office prosecuted a case involving the rape of an eighty-year-old woman. A nineteen-year-old punk broke into her apartment in the middle of the night, robbed her, scared her half to death, and then raped her. The elderly woman had lived in that apartment most of her life. She had raised her children there. Now she was the victim of a particularly heinous crime in her own home.

And do you know what the defendant's investigators did? They went around to her neighbors and asked if they knew about the men she entertained in her apartment. They implied she invited men in for sex. Can you imagine what that did to this elderly woman?

The actions of the defense may have been legal, but they weren't moral. We hand defense lawyers a two-ton smoke machine, and they crank it up. Most jury trials are so thick with smoke it takes a major effort to find the truth. The facts are buried in layers of gray. A defense strategy succeeds when the jury stops thinking about whether the defendant is bad and starts wondering if the victim is bad. There are times when you almost expect to hear the verdict: "We, the jury, find the victim guilty . . ."

Meanwhile, prosecutors, burdened with overwhelming caseloads and limited resources, are not always able to protect victims from being further traumatized. The price of living in a democracy should not be the sanctioned battery of its citizens.

Don't get me wrong. I have no problem with a person's right to be vigorously defended in a court of law. Every person arrested for a crime is entitled to legal representation, but that is someone else's job. My job—and the very essence of who I am—is to make sure the victimizers in our society pay the price for hurting others. What I'm about is settling scores. When someone chooses to victimize another person, I am going to fight like hell to put that person away so he or she can't do it again.

I'm not interested in indicting innocent people—and I get steamed when anyone suggests that prosecutors do this as a matter of course. Last year, a professor from Northwestern University School of Law spoke at a New York State Bar Association conference. He said— to applause—that prosecutors would rather get a death sentence against an innocent person than admit they charged the wrong person with the crime. That was an outrageous remark, and every lawyer in the room— including those who applauded—knew it. I don't know a district attorney in this country who would want a prosecutor like that on staff. Our sacred charge is to pro- tect our communities and reflect the ideals of democracy, not to increase our rate of convictions.

If this sounds unfair or callous or not compassionate enough about the hard-luck stories and extenuating cir- cumstances surrounding some criminals, that's too bad. I don't lose sleep over it. What I do lose sleep over is the fact that, increasingly, our laws, attitudes, and behaviors seem to be veering away from what we say is our moral core as a nation. We say that we exalt good and punish evil, yet we do the opposite.

We turn criminals into celebrities, and view victims with suspicion. We pay lip service to one set of values. Our true feelings are another thing entirely. If we're go- ing to make our communities safer and our society less violent—which is what we all say we want—we're going to have to mean what we say. And if our laws don't work, we should fight to change them. They are not carved in stone. They should reflect our most high-minded instincts.

My personal calling is to punish the predators and to protect the public—to help guarantee the quality of life we're entitled to in a civilized society. That involves balancing the interests of the community at large, the victims, who have paid the dearest price, and the accused. Every case we prosecute places our core values on the line, asking if we have the will to stand as a society in which people are required to follow the law. Every citizen has a stake in this question, and for some it is literally a matter of life and death.

Barry Johnson was sent to jail for his crimes, and in the eyes of many, this was a successful result. Justice was done. The system worked—but did it? While Barry Johnson sits in prison, fantasizing about his victims and having his every need met by the State, what will become of the brave girls who ensured his conviction? Their lives were permanently altered by his deviant hands. Like so many victims, the violation and betrayal they experienced will become the prism through which each new experience is viewed. Every future intimacy will be tainted by the indelible memory of Barry Johnson. We must remember that just because a case is closed, just because a criminal is behind bars, it doesn't mean that our job is finished. As I think of the families irreparably scarred by their encounters with Barry Johnson, I know true justice will not be done until we understand that our obligation doesn't end with punishing the abuser. We must also reach out to heal the victims.

CHAPTER 2

The Deadly Ripple

The devil had been in this apartment. I could feel it as soon as I walked through the door. Evil had been given free rein. It was less than a day after the murders, and the place still vibrated with the horrors that had occurred here.

It was September 4, 2000, and I had just arrived at one of the grisliest murder scenes I had ever encountered. I'd been to plenty of crime scenes before, gruesome scenes where victims had been strangled, or shot, or set on fire, but this was the worst I'd ever seen. Although the bodies had been removed, there was an overwhelming stench of blood and death and fear.

I had decided to go to the Yonkers apartment when I

heard that children were involved. Such violence should never become an abstraction for those of us who prosecute crime. I needed to see for myself the place where twenty-eight-year-old Patricia Torres was slashed to death by her live-in boyfriend, Dennis Alvarez-Hernandez. Where her four-year-old daughter, Ashley, and her seven-year-old son, William, were sliced to shreds as they lay frozen in their beds—their bodies torn apart, their lives ended in a fit of rage. Where her nine-year-old son Vincent had been stabbed again and again in his chest and neck and left for dead. He had managed to survive and was then fighting for his life in a nearby hospital.

The trail of blood told most of the story. A ferocious struggle had taken place in this apartment. It started in the front bedroom. From the kitchen, I could imagine an already wounded Patricia Torres stumbling through the apartment, trying to stop her crazed boyfriend Dennis, pleading and screaming as her children were being sliced open. Her life ended there, on the floor in the children's bedroom. The death room.

The children's room was a snapshot from hell. Blood saturated a bunk bed, both top and bottom. The walls were covered with blood. A blood-soaked comforter was draped from the top bunk. A dark stain covered the floor where Patricia's body was found.

I walked into the bathroom. There was blood smeared all over the floor, blood and feces all over the bathtub and shower. I wondered about that. "Why is there all this feces in the bathtub?" I asked a detective. He shrugged. "They have cats." I shook my head. "No. This is human feces." The detail puzzled me. Nine-year-old Vincent, the only survivor, would later clear up the mystery.

Stabbed eleven times, Vincent had managed to crawl away. His grandparents lived next door. His ten-year-old brother, Rudy, had stayed over at their place the night before, thus avoiding injury or death, and Vincent was determined to get to them. But Vincent, who had some emotional problems to begin with, didn't quite know how to handle the blood covering him. So, even though the murders had just taken place, he went into the shower and tried to wash himself off. He was bleeding heavily and slipping into shock. His bowels let go. It was his feces in the shower.

Still bleeding and wrapped only in a towel, Vincent crawled out a window and went next door. It was early Sunday morning, and his grandmother, Sergia Torres, was already up and preparing for church. She heard the knocking, and opened the door to find Vincent holding the blood-soaked towel around his body, wide-eyed, chalky pale, and crying, "Mommy. Dennis. Mommy. Dennis killed her. On the floor."

Sergia woke her husband Rodolfo and young Rudy, and they went next door and found the bodies. Eleven-year-old Rudy had to know that an angel was watching over him, because he had decided to spend the night with his grandparents.

Dennis Alvarez-Hernandez was picked up at the scene, suffering from knife wounds that were later determined to be superficial and self-inflicted. He told police that Patricia had stabbed her kids, and he had tried to stop her, injuring himself and killing her. He spun this story, confident there were no witnesses to refute it. When he learned Vincent was alive and was accusing him of the stabbings, he broke down and cried.

It was a sunny, warm day. I walked out of the apartment building onto Maple Street. Children were all over the neighborhood playing games. Four-year-old Ashley and seven-year-old William would never get to play again. Vincent would never again think of the happy sounds of Maple Street. He would only remember the horror show.

I went to the hospital to visit Vincent. His upper body was wrapped in bandages, as well as his left hand with which he had desperately tried to fend off the attack. But for the fact that he was a little heavy he would have died, too.

I stood next to Vincent's bed and spoke quietly to him. I told him how brave he was, how courageous for having managed to save himself. He listened carefully to me, but his eyes were pleading. We formed a special bond that day. He was so vulnerable. He needed so much to have someone who could help him, someone who would try to make things right. This little boy would be scarred for life—and not just from the stab wounds. He would forever remember his mother's

screams and the screams of his brother and sister. He
would forever remember fighting for his life, helpless to
stop an enraged Dennis with the knife, coming at him
and plunging it into him again and again.

Vincent was the sole living eyewitness to the events
that had occurred that night. He needed me to make
sure that this vicious murderer would meet certain justice. And I needed Vincent, too, to help me secure that
justice for him. We were bound by our mutual need.

The death penalty was reinstated in New York State in
1995, and we had yet to try a death penalty case in Westchester County. There have been ten death penalty–
eligible cases, but I have elected to seek life without
parole in all of those cases. Now the determination had
to be made whether or not Dennis Alvarez-Hernandez,
twenty-two, should pay for his crime with his life.

If we were going to go forward with the death penalty on this case, I would need to learn everything there
was to know about this defendant. Patricia Torres had a
large and loving family and they were eager to help.

The facts began coming together. It painted a picture
of an extremely jealous, abusive man whose rage had
been fueled by alcohol. Two months before the slayings,
he had tried to run Patricia over with a car after they had
argued outside of a local nightclub. An eyewitness said
it was clear he really intended to hit her with the car.
Alvarez-Hernandez drove up on the sidewalk and was

speeding toward Patricia when the club's bouncer pulled her out of the way.

Neighbors said the couple frequently fought. In court testimony, others said Alvarez-Hernandez was constantly telling people he was going to kill Patricia, boasting, "If she's not mine, she's not going to be anybody's."

It fit right into the pattern. He was always blaming her for their problems, and he knew how to make her pay. He used her kids. He hurt and took away what was most important to her. Then he killed her. It was typical of violent domestic abuse. I had seen variations of it a hundred times. But before I could go forward with a death penalty prosecution, I had to make sure there wasn't a history of mental illness or other extenuating circumstance lurking in Alvarez-Hernandez's past. Was there anything that his defense could use to exonerate him of responsibility for his actions?

Turning to my team, I sent two of my best homicide investigators, Eddie Murphy and Luis Velez, to Alvarez-Hernandez's hometown in Honduras. I wanted them to find out what they could about the defendant. The investigators contacted the Honduran police, who took them into the town where Alvarez-Hernandez had been raised. They were able to establish through family and friends that he didn't have any prior history of mental illness. He had been a regular kid. He had been raised in a relatively functional family. As he grew older, Alvarez-Hernandez had become something of a thug, and he hung out with violent people. He had once been shot in the leg. Then he made his way to the States and into Patricia Torres's life. My investigators returned and reported their findings. Now I knew that we could go forward and seek the death penalty. But there were a number of considerations.

The death penalty evokes a knee-jerk reaction on the part of many people, both pro and con. Opponents can't understand why it would ever be considered. Those who support it often can't understand why it is so rarely sought, even in the most serious of crimes.

The answer is clear. Death penalty cases are extremely difficult to prosecute. They strain the resources of a district attorney's office and the courts. The entire process involves long, protracted battles. The prosecutor's case has to be impeccable, and even then New York's juries are famously ambivalent about the death penalty. Of the forty-three death penalty cases prosecuted in New York State since 1995, only six have resulted in the accused being sentenced to death.

There was no question in my mind that Dennis Alvarez-Hernandez deserved death. But I had to weigh many other factors. The only eyewitness was a troubled, traumatized young boy. How would Vincent comport himself as a witness on the stand? How would the other side treat him? What would the overall defense strategy be? How long would it take to interview and seat a death penalty–qualified jury?

Meanwhile, I began hearing the predictable murmurs in the media and out in the community—the stitching together of a quilt of excuses, all of the reasons why Alvarez-Hernandez wasn't evil, only pathetic. He had been drunk. He hadn't known what he was doing. Now he was sorry. He was repentant.

We all want to believe that people desire justice, at least in theory. It's just that the reality of seeking and receiving justice is such a complex, difficult matter. It's hard for the people who view this process from the outside to keep their focus on the victims. Whenever the newspapers wrote anything about the case, there seemed to be a sympathetic attitude taken toward the alleged murderer. They wrote about how very young Alvarez-Hernandez was—only twenty-two at the time of the murders.

They didn't write very much about four-year-old Ashley, who was eviscerated by this man and left with her guts spilling out of her body. They didn't write all that much about seven-year-old William either, whose blood and remains were splattered on the walls next to his bunk bed. They hardly ever mentioned Vincent, who witnessed this horror show and almost died. Or about the mother, Patricia, only twenty-eight years old, who was forced to watch her children die just before her own life was ended with a final plunge of the knife. So, yes, people may say they want justice. Some of them may want revenge. But too often a discreet veil is drawn over the gruesome reality of the crime.

As an explanation for what had happened, I heard that Alvarez-Hernandez was drunk. I didn't care if he was drunk. What did that have to do with his culpability? It didn't remove the knife from his hand. Did his drunkenness free him of responsibility, absolve him of murder? I was told that he was truly sorry. He even tried to commit suicide in jail. Honestly, I didn't believe he was sorry for his actions. He was only sorry that he was caught. More than a few people actually suggested that these murders weren't really heinous enough for the death penalty. Why? Because the victims weren't strangers to him. Because, you see, he wasn't a serial murderer. Because, you see, Patricia was his girlfriend, and maybe she wasn't so innocent.

It baffled me to hear this constant chorus of forgiveness. I wanted all of those people to have been with me the day after the murders, when I went to that apartment on Maple Street in Yonkers. I wanted them to see the blood and smell the fear and the death. I wanted them to have gone to the hospital with me and seen Vincent swathed in bandages, his eyes pleading for help, pleading to erase the horrors he'd experienced and witnessed. Then I wanted to hear them sing their hosanna of redemption and forgiveness for the murderer who'd attacked him and killed his mother and brother and sister.

Why are we so forgiving of violent criminals? Why do we look so hard for excuses? Why do we try to find ways to blame the victim? I heard people say, "How do you know she didn't stab her kids?" It didn't matter to them that Patricia Torres had been a good mother who took her children to the pediatrician and the dentist, who took Vincent to a therapist. They didn't know how hard she fought to save her children. In spite of many stab wounds, she stumbled through the apartment, trying to reach her babies before they were murdered. She died next to their bed, her efforts futile. Who would speak for Patricia when people flocked to forgive the murderer?

As the evidence mounted against Alvarez-Hernandez, his attorney let it be known that his client would accept a plea-bargained deal for life without parole. It was supposed to be an offer we couldn't refuse.

He would pay dearly for his crime, the victims would have closure, and the state would be spared the expense of a trial. For me, the call wasn't so simple. I had to consider not only what was just for the victims, but what was best for the community. There is a naive supposition that once we lock up a brutal murderer his reign of terror is finally over. That is not true. Murderers kill while in prison, too. There are inmate-on-inmate killings. There are inmate-on-officer killings. Violent criminals don't become gentle once they've been imprisoned.

I've always been haunted by the story of Donna Payant, who was an officer in the New York State Department of Corrections when she was murdered by an inmate named Lemuel Smith in 1981. Smith was an especially depraved persistent felony offender. In 1976, while robbing a religious goods store in Albany, he stabbed employees Robert Hederman and Margaret Byron several times in the chest. He then slit each of their throats, killing them both. Before he was finally apprehended, Smith committed a series of other brutal crimes. After confessing to all of them, Smith was convicted of robbery and kidnapping in Schenectady County, of rape in Saratoga County, and in 1979 he was convicted of the Albany murders of Robert Hederman and Margaret Byron.

In other states, the Hederman-Byron double murder case would have ended in a sentence of death. Under New York's current law, a multiple killing such as this one could result in a death sentence, but no such penalty existed in New York in 1979 for the crimes Lemuel Smith had committed. Only one portion of New York's old death penalty statute had survived to that point, the mandatory death sentence for anyone committing murder while serving a term of life imprisonment. Smith didn't meet the criteria—yet.

Incarcerated at the Greenhaven Correctional Facility in Stormville, New York, Smith was not on death row. He was a member of the general prison population assigned to work, ironically enough, in the Catholic chaplain's office. There he encountered a corrections officer, Donna Payant, and on May 15, 1981, Lemuel Smith raped and beat her, bit her on the breast, and strangled her. He wrapped Payant's body in plastic bags, placed her in a fifty-five gallon waste drum, and carted her off to a Dumpster. Her body was found the next day among the garbage transported from the prison to a landfill.

Because he was serving a life sentence at the time of his latest crime, Lemuel Smith was sentenced to death for Donna Payant's murder. But in 1984, New York's highest court, the Court of Appeals declared this statute, as well as Smith's death sentence, unconstitutional. He received another prison sentence of twenty-five years to life for the murder of Donna Payant, and he lives to someday kill again.

When we consider whether the death penalty is a force for good, we should remember Lemuel Smith. The question isn't whether or not Smith should have received the death penalty for killing Donna Payant, but whether he should have been sentenced to death for slaughtering Robert Hederman and Margaret Bryon—thus sparing Payant's life.

Why is the United States in the minority of Western nations in utilizing capital punishment? Maybe it's because we are not like other Western nations. The American murder rate is four times that of Italy, nine times that of England, eleven times that of Japan. Our rape rate is fifteen times that of England, twenty-three times that of Italy, and twenty-six times that of Japan. There is no accurate model for America. We cannot be guided by what other countries do.

There is evidence that the death penalty does act as a deterrent. In January 2001, three professors from Emory

University published the results of the most comprehensive investigation ever made on capital punishment as a deterrent, using data from every one of the 3,054 counties in the United States, something that had never been done before. They examined crime trends from 1977 through 1996, analyzing the impact of capital punishment. The results indicate that each execution may in fact deter an average of eighteen homicides. But deterrence is only one reason for the death penalty. It's not the only reason.

I believe the principal purpose of the death penalty is neither to exact vengeance nor to deter those who would never have taken a life. It is to prevent those who have killed and who continue to exhibit no regard for human life from killing again. What is more valuable than that? If you commit ultimate crimes you should forfeit not only your right to walk freely among the rest of us, but also your right to breathe our air, eat our food, and share our space on this earth. We should not be required to endure your existence for a moment longer than is absolutely necessary. We should be allowed to purge our sensibilities of you.

Those who oppose the death penalty argue that it is wrong to punish killers by becoming killers ourselves, but not all killings are the same. Some acts inflicting death are right and just, others are unspeakable atrocities. When we blur the line between the two by refusing to make moral distinctions, we devalue our own morality.

We had spent months examining the evidence and evaluating the case. It was time for a decision. If Alvarez-Hernandez didn't deserve death, who did? It finally came down to that. Seeking the death penalty seemed to be the right thing to do.

But one further step was needed. I had to discuss this with Patricia Torres's family.

They gathered around the table in my conference room. Patricia's parents were crushed. Their bodies literally sagged with the terrible burden. They would have to bear this pain for the rest of their lives. This young man with whom their daughter became involved not only abused her, but ultimately destroyed her and their grandchildren.

I looked into their sad faces. "I am considering seeking the death penalty for Dennis," I told them. "But as the family of the victims, you have a right to be heard on this. Before I decide, I want to know what your position is." As we discussed the matter at length, I watched their faces harden into certainty. Their unanimous decision was death.

On May 3, 2001, I announced the decision. We would seek the death penalty against Dennis Alvarez-Hernandez.

As the trial approached, the defense offered to make a deal. Alvarez-Hernandez would plead guilty in exchange for a life sentence. This wasn't much of a concession on his part. It was practically a given that, if convicted, he'd spend the rest of his life in prison. I hadn't sought the death penalty in order to squeeze out a plea deal. I sought the death penalty because I thought it was justified. I rejected the offer.

New York's Capital Defender's Office, which didn't represent Alvarez-Hernandez but was assisting in his defense, commissioned a public opinion poll, at State expense, in an attempt to convince me that voters in the county would exact a political price if I persisted in seeking the death penalty. I never saw the full results of the poll. The Capital Defender's Office disclosed only selected portions. I knew one thing, though. I hadn't taken a poll to help me decide whether to seek the death penalty, and I wasn't going to let poll results determine my actions now.

Thirty-one months after the slayings of Patricia Torres and her children, the trial of Dennis Alvarez-Hernandez was under way before Judge Kenneth Lange. It had taken seven months to seat a jury. The defense position was that Alvarez-Hernandez had committed the murders in an intoxicated state. He didn't know what he was doing, and therefore had not formed the intent necessary for First-Degree Murder.

The star witness would be Vincent, now eleven, still fragile, still healing from emotional and physical wounds. Vincent begged me to come to court the day he testified

and I promised him I would. I had made a point of being there for Vincent throughout this whole process,
and I knew he depended on me.

On April 12, 2003, the day he would testify, I sought
Vincent out before court. His face lit up when he saw
me, and he threw his arms around me. "Are you worried?" I asked as I hugged him. He shook his head no.
"Just tell the truth," I advised him.

With the jury still out of the room, Vincent took the
stand so the judge could ask him a few questions and determine that he understood what he was about to do.
Vincent looked nervous, but he spoke into the micro-
phone with a loud, clear voice. The judge asked him,
"When it is something important, Vincent, does it make
any difference whether you tell the truth or you don't?"
Vincent looked puzzled. "I don't know what you
mean," he answered.

The judge smiled. "Okay. I don't blame you. Is there
any difference between telling the truth, like when you
discuss what kind of candy bar you like, as opposed to
whether the building is on fire and there is a danger?"

"I will tell the truth if the building is on fire," Vincent replied.

"Why is that?" the judge asked.

"Because," Vincent said firmly, "I don't want any of
my family to die."

Satisfied that Vincent would be able to testify truthfully, the judge asked him to step down and wait outside

while he conferred with the attorneys. Before proceeding, the defense attorney, Robert Aiello, made an odd request of the judge. Concerned that Vincent was an extremely sympathetic witness, and therefore damaging to the defendant, he asked the judge to restrain the prosecution from allowing Vincent's testimony to be turned into a sympathy show. He wanted the prosecution barred from saying things like, "This is the hard part," or, "This must be difficult for you." He was worried that the jury would be unreasonably prejudiced by the sight of this young victim and the truth he would speak. A part of me wanted to scream, "Your client chose his victims; we didn't. He tried to kill this boy, and now you want to treat his victim without a shred of decency."

When the jury was seated, the lead prosecutor, Patricia Murphy, began taking Vincent through the events of those terrible hours on September 3, 2000. Dennis Alvarez-Hernandez sat at the defense table looking downward. Murphy kept Vincent's eyes on her so he wouldn't have to look the defendant in the face. Aiello stipulated that the defendant was in the room to prevent whatever drama might occur when an eleven-year-old pointed to the murderer of his mother and siblings.

But, as Vincent was telling his story, he suddenly stopped speaking and sat up a little taller in his seat. "Can I say where he is?" he demanded in a loud voice.

Murphy stepped back. "You want to?" she asked. "You want to point to him? Very well."

You could feel a chill go through the courtroom as

Vincent pointed his finger at Alvarez-Hernandez. Vincent's face was beet red with rage as he stared at the man who had destroyed his family. It was mesmerizing.

Judge Lange ordered a five-minute break and the jury was hustled out of the room. After the break the air in the courtroom was still charged. Dennis Alvarez-Hernandez sat at the defense table with tears streaming down his face. The judge told Aiello he would wait to bring the jury in until his client had composed himself. He replied that a delay wasn't necessary. His game plan was clear. Although he hadn't wanted the jury to feel sympathy for Vincent, he was eager for them to see his client crying. He knew that the first instinct of every person would be to think, "Oh, he's remorseful."

What was the true reason for his tears? Were they the product of shame for what he had done, or was he crying out of regret that the little boy he had stabbed nine times and left for dead had survived to point the finger of blame at him?

When the jury was brought back into the courtroom and seated, Patricia Murphy announced that she had no more questions for Vincent. There were no questions from the defense, and Vincent was excused. He stepped down from the witness box and walked across the courtroom, his back straight with satisfaction and dignity.

It took jurors only four hours of deliberation over two days to find Dennis Alvarez-Hernandez guilty of six counts of First-Degree Murder, three counts of Second-Degree Murder, one count of Second-Degree Attempted

Murder, and one count of Attempted Assault in the killings of Patricia Torres and her two children, as well as Vincent's near-fatal wounding.

In death penalty trials, the guilt phase is separated from the penalty phase. A week after the verdict, jurors returned to consider whether Alvarez-Hernandez would be sentenced to death by lethal injection. During this part of the trial, they would be asked to weigh aggravating factors against mitigating factors, and all twelve would have to reach unanimous agreement for the death penalty to be imposed. In his instructions to the jury, Judge Lange told them that if they could not reach a unanimous decision for the death penalty, he would sentence Alvarez-Hernandez to 115 years or more, assuring that the defendant would never spend a day of his life in freedom.

In New York, where victim-impact evidence is not allowed, the penalty part of the trial is really the defendant's show, and Alvarez-Hernandez's lawyers made the most of the opportunity. They spoke poetically about the defendant's youth. They said he loved the victims. They said he was remorseful. They called witnesses to the stand to testify to his character. They showed videotaped interviews with his grandmother and aunt, speaking from their home in Honduras. In a dramatic finale, Alvarez-Hernandez read a prepared speech to the jury— a plea for mercy. The man who did not testify during the guilt phase, who would not agree to be questioned under oath about his actions on that fateful night, was now allowed to give an unsworn statement—what amounted to a murderer's impact statement. He cried rivers of tears as he told the jury how his own actions had devastated him and his family. Was he telling the truth? Was he lying? We will never know, as we had no right to cross-examine him.

And what of the victims? What of the victims' family? They were forced to remain silent. The jury would not hear about their pain. It would not hear about their daily struggle with the void left by these murders. It was obscene.

After only a day of deliberation, the jury announced that it was unable to reach a unanimous agreement on a sentence of death. Judge Lange could have sent them back to continue deliberations, and the prosecution urged him to do so, but he denied the motion, saying curtly, "The law allows them to disagree."

That's not quite right. New York law recognizes the possibility that jurors may fail to reach unanimity on a sentence of death versus life without parole. Yet it assumes that jurors will be given ample opportunity to try. Was one day an ample opportunity? Had it not been the Friday before the Memorial Day weekend, would it have been considered ample?

Just like that, it was over. Patricia Torres's family slumped in defeat. They could not hold back the tears. Outside the courthouse, thirteen-year-old Rudy, old beyond his years, struggled not to cry as he told reporters of his heartbreak. "What happened today in this courtroom was injustice," he said. "His family asked for mercy, but when my mother asked for mercy, instead he killed." Choking on his words, Rudy made an eloquent statement of the impact on his family—the statement jurors were not allowed to hear. "Dennis will be in prison every day, and this guy's family has the chance to see him. But for us, on special occasions, Mother's Day, Christmas, we go to the cemetery."

You toss a stone into a pond and it creates an ever-widening ripple. Acts of violence, like stones tossed in a pond, create permanent ripples, spreading far beyond the immediate victims. Long after the work of the courts is finished, long after the public's attention has moved on to other stories, long after Patricia Torres and her children are relegated to the newspaper archives, the ripples caused by their murders will continue to create resounding effects.

The surviving victims—Vincent and his older brother Rudy—will, for the rest of their lives, comprehend everything they experience through the blood-tinged prism of this singularly traumatic event. They are permanently scarred. Justice can't change that. What we can change is the momentum of violence in our society.

We can fulfill the social contract, never faltering in our will to punish those who rob our families and communities of peace. We must be willing to let the veil drop so that we can look fully into the face of evil. We must put away the excuses—it was an accident, he was drunk, she didn't mean it, it was a moment of passion, he had a tough childhood, he's sorry—and demand justice. This is our obligation as a society and as a criminal justice system. I never doubt our rectitude. I just remember a warm September day on Maple Street. I remember Patricia Torres and her children. Then I think of Rudy's words, and imagine Rudy and Vincent visiting the graves of their mother and little brother and sister. That's all I need to do.

CHAPTER 3

Hell-Bent

I learned to fight from my mother. In the bucolic upstate town of Elmira, New York, where my parents
settled after they were married, Esther Ferris was a strik-
ing presence. She was both stunningly beautiful and
strong-willed. She never hesitated to speak her mind. I
can still vividly remember her sticking up for complete
strangers—an elderly woman being mistreated in a su-
permarket, a neighborhood kid being bullied. Her big
brown eyes flashing with indignation, she would confront the offender head-on, her words clear and bitingly
articulate, in spite of her accent.

My mother wasn't a formally educated woman, but
she had a natural intelligence and a strong sense of jus-

tice. When she talked about the difference between right and wrong she wasn't just mouthing words. Her values were tangibly reflected in her actions.

As a young girl, I couldn't fully appreciate just how remarkable my mother's strong sense of self-esteem was. Her own upbringing had been designed to crush her independent spirit. My mother was born in this country to a first generation Lebanese-American mother and a Lebanese immigrant father, who became a citizen and immediately joined the Navy. As far as my grandfather was concerned, my grandmother had one essential duty as his wife: to bear him male offspring. Instead, in rapid succession, she blessed him with four daughters. Grandfather promptly divorced grandmother, and sent the daughters to live with relatives in Lebanon.

Although my mother was born an American citizen, she was sent to far distant Lebanon when she was five years old. The girls were reared by their father's influential, wealthy brother and lived at his home in Beirut. In that environment, her subservient position was reinforced each and every day. It was the nature of the culture.

My grandfather soon remarried, and his second wife promptly bore him two sons. He rarely communicated with his first wife and four daughters. Then, while serving in the Navy during World War II, he met Leo Ferris, a second-generation Lebanese American from Scranton, Pennsylvania. When my grandfather told Ferris that he had a beautiful daughter living in Lebanon, the young sailor was interested. After the war ended he traveled to Lebanon, fell in love with my mother, Esther, and they eloped. He brought her home with him to America as his wife.

My parents soon moved to Elmira, where my grandfather had a very successful business. They settled into a comfortable middle-class life, and they created the loving, stable environment that allowed my sister and me to thrive. My mother reached out and reconciled with her father, even though he had abandoned her as a young girl. That sweetness of character and charity of spirit was a part of her nature, but she never allowed anyone to treat her like a second-class citizen again.

She impressed upon me throughout my childhood that I had to fight for myself, and I had to help those who were not strong enough to fight for themselves. It was the main reason I became a lawyer. I'm sure it has a lot to do with my sense of outrage every time I learn that a woman has been beaten senseless, stabbed, raped, shot, or thrown off the roof of a building by yet another man who, desperate for some old-fashioned power and control, goes berserk.

When a man is hell-bent on hurting his wife or girlfriend, there's not much we can do to stop him. At least, not the way the system is set up right now. This is one of the dirtiest secrets in our great nation. Women are dying every day because we're not protecting them. It's a crime.

What's really galling is that we have the power to prevent it. These aren't random acts of violence. They're utterly predictable. A 2002 FBI report states that domestic violence is the leading cause of injury to women between the ages of fifteen and forty-four—more than car accidents, muggings, and rapes combined. According to the National Violence Against Women Survey, more than 1.5 million women are raped or violently assaulted by a husband, ex-husband, or boyfriend every year. Most disturbing is a recent report stating that homicide is the leading cause of death for pregnant women— twice the rate of medical fatalities.

In the civil war that rages in homes across America, women die quietly, silent witnesses to our indifference. They don't capture our attention because they are disenfranchised, or poor, or weak, or because they loathe themselves. They don't think they're worthy of being heard. A national study concluded that only twenty-five percent of all domestic violence is reported to the police. The majority of nonreporters said they didn't think the police would or could do anything to help them.

When I started out as a young prosecutor in 1975 I was blind to the issue of domestic violence. It wasn't even on my radar screen. I was in the Appeals Bureau, and one of the first homicide cases I handled during my first year involved domestic violence. My job was to write the state's response to an appeal by two men convicted of killing the wife of one of them. David Safian and Robert Miner had been convicted by a jury of intentional murder. They, like all convicts, were entitled to appeal the conviction to a higher court. I would study the records and write the prosecution's response to the defense appeal.

I lugged the heavy box containing trial transcripts, police and autopsy reports, and other materials into my office and started going through them. In a brown manila envelope I found the autopsy photos and spread them out in front of me. I stared at them for a long time.

Debbie Safian had been a beautiful girl. Her long brown hair shined even in death. She was only twenty-one when she died, already the mother of two children, one of them from a previous relationship. She was struggling to make ends meet, but she had guts. She'd left her abusive husband, David. She was going to school during the day and waitressing at night—working hard to create a better life for herself and her children.

In the sterile setting of the autopsy, the violence that had ended Debbie's life was muted. The blood that flowed in rivers from twenty-one stab wounds had been washed away. Only the wounds themselves were visible, clean slashes across her breasts, her abdomen, her face. A pattern of wounds on her arms and hands showed how she had fought for her life.

What was the price of Debbie's life? One thousand dollars cash, paid by David Safian to Robert Miner, a seventeen-year-old boy. One thousand dollars because Robert wanted to buy a used motorcycle and David wanted to end the existence of the woman who had dared to leave him.

Debbie Safian's murder was a horrifying eye-opener for me. That a man could be so cool in arranging for the slaughter of his wife and the mother of his child was incomprehensible. I poured my heart and soul into writing the appeal response, and I was gratified when the conviction was affirmed and Safian and Miner remained behind bars. But Debbie Safian haunted me. I began to read everything I could find on the subject of domestic violence. My naiveté was shattered as I learned that Debbie's story was all too common, and there was practically no recourse for women caught in the same bind.

Thirty years ago battered women weren't protected by law. They were helpless. The social contract did not include them. They were inconsequential; they weren't a lobbying group. Most of them never even spoke up. People said, "Why don't they just leave?" I had said it myself. At first, I didn't get it, but I would soon learn.

The coldness of the law, its brutal indifference, appalled me. A man could shoot, stab, beat, or brutalize his wife with no consequences. A woman could not charge her husband with rape. These were not considered crimes. There was a flawed notion that violence and rape in the home were beyond the reach of the law, protected by a family's right to privacy. If the law intervened at all, the case would be reported and referred to the Family Court. At the time, the legislated purpose and intent of the Family Court was to keep families together.

What were we thinking? A man beats his wife, rapes her, and terrorizes his children, and our response was, "What can we do to keep this family together?" It was a tragic farce. How could we be so focused on stranger violence, without any regard for the family violence that ultimately spills out onto the street?

It took until 1977 before the New York State Legislature passed a law making domestic assault a crime. Like most states, we were slow to come to an understanding of the criminal nature of family violence. The new law meant that violent acts within the immediate family were no longer the sole domain of Family Court. We could now bring them into criminal court and prosecute them with the same rigor applied to stranger assaults.

That was exactly what I intended to do, although the idea of taking domestic abusers to court did not sit well with everyone. Many people just didn't believe these cases were criminal, and they didn't want to spend the limited resources of our office on "family problems."

In 1978, when the Law Enforcement Assistance Administration made federal money available for pilot Domestic Violence Prosecution Units, the Westchester County DA's office bid for the grant. We were one of four offices in the entire country approved for the project, and I became chief of the office, with three aides and a criminal investigator.

In my boss's opinion, 90 percent of our work was social services. His attitude pervaded our office and the courts. Time and again, I'd go to court and judges would bark at me, "Why don't you get a real case, Ms. Pirro?" Or they'd throw the case out with an admonishment to stop wasting the court's time. I remember one judge in particular who would look at a woman standing before him with a black eye and a swollen jaw, and say, "Ma'am, you don't belong here. This is a criminal court, not a family court." In those instances when we got all the way to a jury, I repeatedly heard, "What did she do to make him so mad?"

It was a constant battle. Judges at the time were extremely reluctant to issue orders of protection in domestic-violence cases. Frequently we'd face puzzled judges who would say, "How can we order him out of the house? He's paying the mortgage." They'd get bogged down, worrying about who was going to write the order, or who was going to serve the order. In frustration, I decided to act. I began creating my own orders, written on the District Attorney's office stationery, which I would hand out to battered women. They didn't have the force of law, but they provided a small extra layer of protection. I told women that if they had to call the police, they should show the orders to the officers who responded. It would let them know a woman had made prior complaints, and that our office found her credible.

I recognized immediately that there was another enormous impediment to our work. Women who had been battered had a problem coming to our office, which was in the courthouse. It was intimidating to them, and humiliating. I appealed to Vergari. I said, "When these women come in, they're extremely upset. They need a place where they can be comfortable and feel safe. They're embarrassed to walk through the courthouse with bruised faces." A storefront office, directly accessible to the street, was the answer. It wasn't easy, but we eventually got our storefront—across the street from the courthouse.

I recruited volunteers to decorate the office, put in a play area for the children, and made it a more welcoming atmosphere. We set up a network of support in the community, and connected with the broader movement that was developing at that time. The women and children started coming in. Within two years we were handling more than two thousand cases.

The numbers proved my point. Domestic violence wasn't a rare occurrence. It was an epidemic. Yet too many people, including those in law enforcement, didn't believe it was a serious matter. Worse still, they treated it like a joke. There was a saying at the time, "Every woman should be taken with a grain of assault." How could such a sentiment produce laughs?

I was getting educated. I learned that victims of domestic violence didn't always come to the program all shiny and sympathetic. Many of the women had severe problems—lack of economic resources, poor self-esteem, ignorance, drugs, alcohol. I had to accept them as victims and try to understand that they were where they were because of their situation.

Janet Petit was such a woman. On the day she hobbled into our office she had been beaten so badly it was painful to look at her. I'd never seen anything like it. In a shy voice she told me the police wouldn't arrest her husband. That made no sense to me, and I placed a call. "Why didn't you arrest this woman's husband?" I asked the officer. "He beat her within an inch of her life."

The policeman sighed, a world-weary sound. "Well, you know, she's a bad drunk. She falls down a lot."

"Oh, come on," I said. "Explain to me what kind of fall leaves welts and bruises under your arms or on the backs of your legs. What kind of a fall leaves choke marks around your neck?"

I convinced Janet to press charges against her husband. The attempts to help her get temporary housing weren't successful. The shelters wouldn't accept Janet because she had a drinking problem. She had no choice but to stay with the husband who beat her. While we waited to go to trial, I worked with Janet and tried to restore her confidence. I repeatedly assured her that going to trial was the right thing to do. On the day of the trial, with everyone gathered in the courtroom, there was only one obstacle to seeking justice: Janet. There was no sign of her. She showed up two hours late. She was stinking drunk.

The judge motioned her husband's lawyer and me to approach the bench. He was disgusted. "Ms. Pirro," he said, "your witness is obviously not up to testifying. I'm going to dismiss this case, and I strongly suggest that you think hard before you waste the court's time again on these matters."

I was angry with the judge, but most of all I was angry with Janet. I was mad at Janet for not conforming to the needs of the system, when I should have been mad at the system for being unable to meet Janet's needs. I understand now. I didn't get it back then.

Janet drank. There were probably a thousand reasons why she did. She drank because nobody believed her. Nobody cared. She drank because she was miserable, imperfect. Her husband beat her. He threatened to strangle her and burn her. But she was too impaired for the system to make a place for her and to protect her rights. How could Janet believe in us when we had proven time and again that we couldn't or wouldn't help her? We couldn't even find a temporary home for her. Once her case was dismissed, she faded back into the community and I never saw her again.

A year later, a detective from Dade County, Florida, visited me in my office. My card had been found among the possessions of a woman who was killed by her husband in Florida. It was Janet. She had been strangled and burned. My heart sank with the sickening realization that I was part of the system that had failed her. I had been furious with Janet for not believing in our power to help her. I wanted her to feel hope when, in truth, she had little to hope for. Our office cooperated with Florida authorities, and Janet's husband was convicted. She got her justice—in death.

Many times women didn't want to press charges, didn't want to testify. Some people couldn't understand why a woman would refuse to press charges after an assault. They used this refusal as a way to blame the victim, arguing that the law couldn't help her if she wouldn't help herself. That point of view was very limited. There were a million reasons why women didn't press charges, but the bottom line was simple and clear. They didn't trust the system to protect them.

If they'd ever tried to get help, they knew what happened when the police, the courts, and the social services agencies got involved in your life. Even though you were the victim, the consequences could be grave. Women who pressed charges against violent husbands or partners risked having their children taken away from them and placed in foster care. Can you imagine anything more punitive?

If you report that you are a victim of battery, not only will we not protect you, but we'll punish you by taking your children away. It wouldn't be until 2002, when Judge Jack B. Weinstein delivered a scathing ruling in federal district court in New York, that the practice was ended. As Judge Weinstein wrote, "When ACS [the Administration for Children's Services] prosecutes a mother for neglecting her child when she has done nothing but suffer battery at the hands of another . . . it infers from the fact that a woman has been beaten and humiliated that she has permitted or encouraged her own abuse. It desecrates fundamental precepts of justice to blame a crime on the victim."

Judge Weinstein's ruling was long overdue. When I was working with battered women in the 1980s, the penalty for complaining could be worse than the abuse. And the experience was almost always demeaning.

I saw plenty of women who did press charges and were brave enough to go to court. They would sit for hours, shifting uncomfortably on the hard benches, waiting for their cases to be called. Their husbands would show up with dismissive lawyers, who would portray the women as crazy, neurotic, the ones who started it. Their abusers would appear calm and reasonable before judges, hiding the fury that would soon be turned again on their victims. Maybe they'd be thrown into jail for twenty-four hours, or get off with a stern lecture by the judge. You'd have to be an idiot not to see what was coming.

Often my eyes locked with those of a woman who knew she had lost, a woman who knew what violence lay in store for her even as her abuser was being handcuffed and led off to serve a couple of days' time for her last beating. I remember a woman who murmured hopelessly of the man who repeatedly threatened to kill her, "I wish he'd just get it over with." He did—shortly after being released from jail.

I rarely met an abused woman who wasn't ambivalent about pressing charges against her husband or boyfriend, especially if he was the father of her children. She didn't want to expose him. She wanted to give him another chance. She was pressured by family members who faulted her for the discord. Usually, she still loved him. Always, there was a hope that the situation wasn't as bad as it seemed. Emotionally crushed, many women had learned to accept their abusers' foul reasoning as truth. In their own minds, they thought they did deserve it.

Unfortunately, at that time the police weren't required to arrest a person who had committed an act of domestic violence. An abused woman was required to press charges, while a stranger who attacked a woman on the street would be arrested whether the woman pressed charges or not. Why should it be any different when the assault came from an intimate? It was unfair to put the onus on the victims. By forcing these women to make the decision about whether their abusers would be arrested, the police inadvertently placed them in greater danger, once the men were released from custody. I got involved with organizations lobbying for a mandatory arrest law, but New York State would not pass one until 1994. Today, most states have mandatory arrest laws for domestic assaults.

Even when women pressed charges and we took

their cases to criminal court it was common for them to change their minds. They were so fearful of their abusers or so deep in their denial of the problem that they refused to come to court. I heard horribly beaten women say, "If you put me on the stand I'm going to testify that he didn't hit me."

We started moving forward with prosecutions without seeking testimony from the victims. Diane Smith* was a twenty-one-year-old woman whose thirty-one-year-old boyfriend, Robert Snyder, had a history of both beating and sexually assaulting her. Once, he held her hostage at her sister's apartment for several days. Finally, on August 7, 1989, he tried to kill her. He threatened her with a knife and forced her to the roof of his building, where he bludgeoned her with a ball-peen hammer, and left her for dead. She survived, although her injuries required a metal plate to be placed in her skull.

As the trial neared, Diane announced that she wouldn't testify against her boyfriend. At that point I no longer cared. I got the picture. It wasn't just about Diane anymore, it was about the next victim. It was about protecting the community from people who believe they have a right to resolve conflicts with violence. So, Diane Smith sat on the witness stand and testified that her boyfriend had never assaulted her. In fact, she told the jury she fell while she was trying to assault him with a

*Not her real name.

bread knife. The jury didn't believe her. They came back with a conviction for Attempted Murder.

Prosecuting batterers without relying on testimony from their victims was a new strategy that required the retraining and cooperation of the responding police officers. Without direct testimony from the victim, we needed the police to help us prove the cases circumstantially. We began to hold training sessions for officers. I would say to them, "Assume she's a homicide victim. You save the audiotape when she calls the police [this was before the 911 emergency system]. You take photographs of her detailing her injuries. You save her clothing for evidence. You take a written statement. You get witnesses lined up right away." I recognized that it was important to give police officers tools. Early in my tenure as DA, I would provide every police department in the jurisdiction with Polaroid cameras.

Initially, most police officers were loath to get involved in domestic cases. They preferred doing it the old-fashioned way, which usually involved taking the abuser for a walk around the block to calm him down, and having a man-to-man chat with him. They nicknamed our unit the "Tit Patrol" and the "Panty Brigade." These weren't affectionate terms. Over time police officers developed more respect for our office. Once we backed up their arrests with prosecutions and convictions, they could acknowledge our legitimacy.

After the federal grant money for our Domestic Violence Unit dried up we had to do battle to keep the unit in the budget every single year. Year after year, we were cut out of the budget. We were disposable. To stay alive, I learned to galvanize support from women's groups and individuals who cared about our mission.

I guess the resistance shouldn't have surprised me. We were fighting a core value system that was as old as recorded time. In ancient Rome, if a woman talked back to her husband, her name was carved on a brick, which was then used to knock out her teeth. When an idea is so culturally ingrained, it can't be changed overnight.

This mentality is a plague that infects everyone—the abuser, the victim, the police officers, the judges, the juries. It's insidious, destructive, and all-encompassing.

Renee Linton was a victim of the system and of this hardened mentality, and that paved the way for her to be the ultimate victim. I'll never forget Renee—how hard she fought for herself and her children, how hard we fought for her—to no avail.

Renee first walked into our office in January 1986. She wanted to press charges against her husband, Michael, who she was in the process of divorcing. She also wanted an order of protection to keep him away from her and their three children.

Michael Linton had terrorized his family for a long

time. In the summer of 1985, when they were living in North Carolina, Renee had taken the children and fled to New York, after Michael had played a game of Russian roulette with them—pointing a gun at their heads as she and the children cowered in a bedroom. He kept pulling the trigger and laughing when it clicked on an empty chamber. Michael was a former Green Beret, a man who had been trained to kill and to assert control. In his twisted vision, that control extended to Renee and the children.

Leaving Michael only made things worse for Renee. He was still very much in the picture—calling her constantly, threatening her. He told her he was going to kill her so many times that she became numb to his threats. She almost didn't hear the words anymore. The day before she came to our office he had slashed her tires with a large knife. He would then wave the knife in her face, taunting her: "I fixed your business."

I urged Renee to go to a women's shelter in a secret location and she followed my advice. She and her three children spent the next few months in a single room at the shelter. In March 1986, the court granted a final order of protection and warned Michael, "Stay away from Renee and the children or you'll be arrested."

Renee was scared to death of Michael, with good cause. She wasn't an hysteric. She just knew. For the next year, she moved in and out of shelters and apartments, changed jobs three times, and changed her phone number five times. But Michael always found her. He'd call Renee day and night, always with the threats—"I'm going to kill you. I'm going to put you six feet under." On more than one occasion, Renee would look out the window at work and her stomach would clench. There was Michael's car—a custom-painted orange BMW, you couldn't miss it—idling outside.

Early one morning in January 1987, Michael showed up at her apartment door, pounding, yelling, threatening to kill her. This time Renee called the police, but he'd fled by the time they arrived. On January 8, a warrant was issued for Michael's arrest.

When police picked him up on January 14 and informed him he was being arrested for violating the order of protection, Michael was livid. He'd been around the system, and he knew what to expect. "Is she stupid?" he raged, riding in the police car to the station. "I'll be out of here in half an hour. I'll kill that bitch!"

It would be another three weeks before Michael made good on his threat. In the meantime, Renee saw a lawyer, and, at the age of thirty-two she signed her last will and testament. On the evening of February 10, 1987, Michael climbed the fire escape to Renee's apartment. While the children slept in their beds he emptied a gun into the woman he had promised to kill. While she was still alive he stuffed her body into the oven. A detective called to the scene, observing Renee's bullet-riddled body, would compare the intensity of the violence to the aftermath of a commando raid. The autopsy report showed that in addition to thirteen gunshot wounds, Renee suffered second degree burns on her back and lower extremities.

Eluding the authorities, Michael Linton remained on the loose for another four months. His eventual arrest seemed to be a small victory. But, once the criminal justice system got into the act, the same impersonal shroud that had fallen over his dead wife's body fell over her killer's reign of terror.

Because of the rules of evidence, which strictly limit references to matters that are not the result of the specific charged crimes, I was precluded from telling the jury that Michael's three children were so terrified of him that the court had granted an order of protection to keep him away from them. That would be the same order of protection that had proved so ineffective for their dead mother. While Michael was out on bail—yes, he made bail!—the first thing he did was head over to Social Services to find his kids and apply for custody. He was rearrested for breaking yet another order of protection.

After months of contentious hearings we went to trial: The People of the State of New York v. Michael Linton. As I stood in the courtroom, about to make my opening statement, I felt the jury was being cheated because the opening argument would include only part of what I knew to be the truth. I wanted to say, "Let me

tell you what I know." The rules of evidence con-
structed an elaborate safeguard for the defendant that
prevented me from speaking for the victim. Michael's
threats, Renee's words, her pleas, her fear were all
hearsay and were not allowed. At one point, when I had
the audacity to call Renee a decent woman, the defense
objected, and the judge sustained the objection.

The jurors would never hear that Renee Linton told
everyone she knew—her family, her friends, her coworkers, the shelter staffs, prosecutors and investigators in our
office—that Michael Linton told her he was going to
kill her. The jurors wouldn't hear about his constant
threats, the late-night phone calls during which he conducted a macabre countdown: "You've got ten days to
live . . . nine days to live . . . eight days to live." They
wouldn't hear about the time he told her, "I might as
well kill the kids, too. You've contaminated them." They
wouldn't hear about the two years Renee spent on the
run, always to be found by Michael, who prowled the
streets in his orange BMW. "I know he's going to kill
me," Renee said over and over and over again. If our
purpose at trial was a real search for the truth, Renee's
words would have been allowed.

In the end, the jurors were able to discern the truth
through the lengthy testimony of police officers and
others who could provide direct testimony about Michael's actions in the months before Renee's death. On
February 22, 1988, approximately a year to the day that
he stole Renee's life, Michael Linton was convicted of

Intentional Murder and sentenced to twenty-five years to life.

By 1990 I had a reputation in the community as some-one who would fight for women and children. I had two children of my own at that time, and being a mother only deepened my resolve. I believed then, as I do today, that families had a right to be whole. Children deserved to grow up in safe, nurturing environments. Every night when I tucked my children into bed and kissed them goodnight, I said a prayer for the women and children whose nights were punctuated by the terror, anxiety, and panic that accompanied punches, slaps, and threats.

When I was asked to run for a seat on the West-chester County Court I was ambivalent. I didn't want to give up my crusade. Judges are not advocates. They can't take sides. At the same time, after countless appearances in court, I was well aware that the absence of a woman's viewpoint in the judiciary was an imbalance with prac-tical ramifications. Never in the history of Westchester County had a woman been elected a county court judge. I knew, for example, that in my court no man who beat his wife would easily make bail. A guy like Michael Linton, who told police, "I'll be out of here in half an hour. I'll kill that bitch!" would not get a free ride. Many of the groups that had supported our efforts to prosecute batterers urged me to run. So I agreed.

Upon my election, and before assuming my criminal

court responsibilities, I was temporarily assigned to preside at Family Court hearings. The first case I heard then involved failure to pay child support. The guy was months in arrears on his court-ordered monthly payments, and his ex-wife and kids were about to lose their apartment.

I eyed him over the top of the bench. He looked bored and indifferent, and that just infuriated me. It wasn't the first time he'd failed to pay, and his smug attitude was written all over his face. He didn't think anyone could make him pay. We'd see about that. I gestured to his wife, a tired and unkempt young woman sitting at the opposite table. Seated behind her was her mother with the couple's two young children.

I said to him, "Sir, that's your wife, those are your kids. You are responsible for support, and you're not paying it."

He spoke up right away—a big mistake. "Your honor, that's true. But I have an explanation." And before he could utter another word, I cut him off. "You know what?" I said, seething. "You're going to jail."

He stepped back, stunned. His ex-wife burst into tears. There was a clamor in the courtroom. On my right, the court clerk was leaning forward, whispering urgently, "Judge—Judge."

I stood up. "Ten-minute recess," I announced and walked out into the robing room followed by the clerk. She was looking at me as if I was crazy. "Judge," she said, "this isn't criminal court. We don't usually put people in jail here."

My concern was for the petitioner. I directed the clerk to find out why she was crying.

She hurried out and returned moments later, shaking her head in surprise. "Judge, she says she was overcome by emotion. She says no one has ever tried to help her before."

"Okay, that's it, then," I said. We returned to the courtroom where I conferred briefly with my law secretary, who was somewhat bemused by my stance. "Kevan, can I send this guy to jail? I think I can."

Kevan looked uncomfortable. "Well, technically you can. . . ."

"Good." I called the court to order and motioned the man to stand. "You're going to jail."

His eyes widened and I watched the self-assured smirk turn to fear as he started gasping in protest. His lawyer was stunned and told me I couldn't send his client to jail. I gave him my coldest stare. "You've got until tomorrow to come up with the money. All of it."

I could hear his bleating protests all the way down the hall. But guess what? He came up with the money.

Word got out pretty fast that the new judge was going to start putting men in jail if they didn't pay child support. A lot of these guys thought I was crazy, but they usually came up with the money. Once a guy smirked at me. "Judge, if you send me to jail, I'll lose my job and won't be able to pay support. What will that accomplish?" This guy really thought he had me.

"Oh, no," I said. "You're going to keep your job Monday through Friday, and you're going to jail on the weekends. Friday night through Sunday night. And if you stop working, I'll hold you in contempt."

Later that day I got a call from the jail. The warden growled at me, "This is very difficult administratively, checking in, checking out." I told him I didn't care. "It's not my job to make your life easier," I said. I had little patience for the polite customs of the system, and I wasn't interested in doing things a certain way simply because they'd always been done that way before. To me, these were easy calls.

I poured my soul into being a judge, on and off the bench. I hosted a weekly public access show to educate the public about the law. I gave talks to countless community groups. By my second year I was feeling stifled as a judge. I was restless. It went against my nature. At heart I was a crusader. I wanted to fight, not preside. As a judge, you can only make an impact here and there, with individuals. Mostly, you're the referee. In less than two years I was ready for a change.

Around that time, Carl Vergari announced he was retiring after twenty-six years as district attorney, and people started calling me, asking if I would run. I really felt it was the job I was born for, but I hesitated. My children were seven and four. Was it right for my family?

I realized that I had a joint vocation—to my family and to my work. I was no different than millions of women who struggled to balance the needs of their families with the demands of their profession.

Still, when I announced in 1993, I was barraged with questions by the press. "Who is going to take care of your kids?" I was surprised. The issue had not been raised when I ran for county court judge. During the campaign, that question was enthusiastically embraced by my opponent, a man with three kids whose wife was pregnant with a fourth. Nobody was asking him about taking care of his kids.

I was not the first woman, nor, unfortunately, the last to have faced these stereotypes and double standards. I wanted to talk about the issues, about my determination to bring predators to justice and to protect victims. The press wanted to talk about who would be cooking dinner for my children. It was maddening.

Fortunately, the people of Westchester got it. They knew I wouldn't let them down. I was elected by a comfortable margin.

In 2000, when I was serving as president of the New York State District Attorney's Association, I was privileged to make the acquaintance of a lawyer named Charlotte Smallwood. In 1950, at the age of twenty-six, Charlotte became the first woman to be elected district attorney in the state of New York. Now in her seventies and still practicing law, Charlotte enjoyed telling the story of the first time she attended a meeting of the District Attorney's Association. When she was introduced to the well-liquored gathering, the room erupted in whistles and catcalls, which Charlotte took in stride. Meeting Charlotte reminded me of how far women had come. The press might have hounded me about my maternal responsibilities, but no one would dare utter a catcall.

To my delight, I would also discover that being the DA gave me a fresh platform for teaching my children. One day, my five-year-old son Alex asked me, "Mommy, can boys be DA?" I assured him, smiling, "These days, boys can grow up to be anything they want to be."

I first took the oath of office as Westchester County District Attorney at midnight on January 1, 1994. I was exhilarated, filled with a deep sense of belonging in the job. I couldn't wait to get started. That opportunity would come faster than I knew. As I held my hand on the Bible and spoke the words of my oath, an event was occurring a few miles away that would jump-start my tenure and bring into focus everything I was about.

My phone rang shortly before dawn on New Year's Day with the gruesome details of a savage attack. Police had received a call at 3:50 A.M. from a young man named Todd Douglas, who was concerned because his brother Scott had left a cryptic message on his answering machine, indicating something bad had happened. Todd was worried about his sister-in-law, Anne Scripps Douglas, since there was a divorce pending. Todd urged the police to check the house immediately. He'd tried to call, but there was no answer. He also mentioned his fear for Scott and Anne's three-year-old daughter, Victoria.

When the police arrived at the couple's Bronxville home, they tried the door and found it locked. They broke in and searched the house. In the bedroom they found Anne Scripps Douglas unconscious on the bed, the sheets covered with blood. She had been bludgeoned with a claw hammer. Curled protectively next to her body was her terrier puppy. Three-year-old Victoria was asleep in another room. Scott Douglas was nowhere to be found. His BMW was missing.

Anne was rushed to the hospital, barely alive and unable to breathe on her own. She was placed on life support while her family, who had begged her so many times to leave Scott, began a grim vigil by her bed.

Meanwhile, I began my first term as district attorney by setting up a war room in the conference room next to my office. I was determined to get this guy, the type of classic abuser I had prosecuted with single-minded passion during my fifteen years as an assistant district attorney. Anne Scripps Douglas was proof to nonbelievers that domestic violence was not limited to the disadvantaged, where poverty, ignorance, and the daily battle to survive spilled over into violent acts. It was also the domain of the wealthy, where secrecy and shame kept it hidden until it was too late.

Shortly after police had discovered Anne's bludgeoned body, Scott's 1982 BMW, the bloody hammer inside, was found idling on the Tappan Zee Bridge. Did Scott jump off the bridge? Divers were sent into the icy water to look for him. The family and friends of Anne Scripps Douglas told authorities that Scott purchased camping equipment shortly before Christmas and that the car on the Tappan Zee was just a ruse. We had to operate on the assumption that Scott was still alive and hiding. In the coming days, we poured over every scrap of evidence, trying to pinpoint Scott's whereabouts.

As for the details of what had occurred that night, we had a witness. At first, it appeared that little Victoria had slept through the attack and was spared the terrifying sight of her mother's assault. Tragically, this was not true. In tearful confusion, the small girl told us what she saw. "Daddy was giving Mommy so many bad boo-boos," she said. "Daddy gave Mommy many boo-boos. Why was my Mommy wearing paint?"

Anne Scripps Douglas was taken off life support and died a week later. We ended the search of the Hudson River at the same time. Even if Scott had jumped, it wasn't likely that his body would surface before spring. The temperature of the water during the winter months would have prevented the body gases from expanding.

As we continued our investigation, we received fresh details of the last days of Anne Scripps Douglas's life.

She had been terrified of her husband; there was no question of that. In early December, she sought an order of protection, and the court ordered Scott to stop harassing his wife, but allowed him to stay in their home. The situation deteriorated further. After Christmas, Anne returned to court in White Plains, trying to have Scott evicted. There was no judge to see her because of the holidays, even though hers was a real emergency. Defeated, she returned home and placed a claw hammer next to her pillow for protection. That claw hammer would become the murder weapon used by her husband.

We continued to work the case as the icy winter turned into spring. Finally, three months after the event, a railroad employee came upon a floater, miles downstream from the bridge. Dental records confirmed it was Scott's body. A gold watch on his wrist eerily confirmed his hour of death as midnight on New Year's Eve.

The violence that ended Anne Scripps Douglas's life so prematurely left many victims behind, including a three-year-old girl. Months after her mother's death, Victoria asked her grandparents, "Is Mommy an angel in heaven? Does Mommy still have boo-boos on her face?"

How does one answer questions like that? What explanation or assurance could possibly give comfort? What happens to a child whose last sight of her mother was her bloodied, lifeless face? Victoria thought it was war paint. In many ways it was just that.

• • •

As a young prosecutor handling domestic violence cases, I began to notice a whisper in the background that came up too often to ignore. In the course of describing the escalation of violence in their homes, women would mention, "And then he threw the cat against the wall . . ." or, "He kicked the dog until it was bloody." There seemed to be a direct correlation between animal cruelty and violence perpetrated against others. The abuse of a family pet was often the first indicator of domestic violence. It made sense to me, although the connection was not widely acknowledged within law enforcement at the time. As District Attorney, I created an animal-abuse team staffed by specially trained prosecutors who are committed to the prevention of cruelty to animals and the prosecution of the abusers. We prosecuted a man who stabbed his girlfriend's dog thirty-one times in a domestic dispute. We prosecuted another man who, in a fit of rage, threw the family cat out of a window to its death. I was determined to make sure that animal abusers were punished.

At first many people didn't get it. They'd say, "Doesn't the DA have enough human victims—she has to start protecting dogs and cats?" Over time that attitude has changed as professionals in the domestic violence field began to recognize the role that animals play in the dynamics of family violence. A 1997 survey of fifty of the largest shelters for battered women in the United States found that 85 percent of women and 63 percent of children entering shelters reported incidents of pet abuse in the family.

Animal abuse is an example of the ripple effect of family violence. In fact, children who have witnessed domestic violence or who have been the victims of physical or sexual abuse may also become animal abusers themselves, imitating the violence they have seen or experienced. A study conducted in 1995 noted that 32 percent of the pet-owning victims of domestic abuse reported that one or more of their children had hurt or killed a pet.

Many studies conducted during the past twenty-five years have shown that violent offenders frequently have childhood and adolescent histories of severe, repeated animal cruelty. This is particularly true of those who go on to become abusers within their own families—of spouses, children, and elderly parents. In addition, the FBI has determined that a consistent factor among serial killers is a history of killing or torturing animals as children.

I'm an animal lover. Long before I became a prosecutor, I had already figured it out for myself that people who are cruel to animals will be cruel to people, too. They lack humanity. As DA, I believe that when we protect a family pet from violence we may well be protecting the entire family and the community from a vicious predator.

• • •

The first order of government is to protect its citizens. An important part of that process is figuring out where and why we fail. Often, the difference between life and death in a domestic violence case can be as insignificant as one small change—an addition or adjustment to a statute that commissions and experts have called for. There are beaten and bloodied bodies all along the way to the signing of legislation to protect women. Far too often it takes a tragedy to create the impetus to change our laws and enhance our system.

In October 1996 New York Governor George Pataki appointed me to chair a year-long commission to study domestic violence fatalities in the state. Our mandate was to investigate domestic violence–related homicides that had occurred over a seven-year period, and to determine whether those deaths could have been prevented. What were the deficiencies in the courts, law enforcement, and social services that we could correct? We held public hearings, interviewed victims, and heard testimony from medical personnel, law enforcement officers, shelter staff, social services administrators, psychiatrists, marriage counselors, prison inmates, and experts on family violence.

Our findings were extremely troubling, but they confirmed what many of us already knew. Before their murders, these women often pounded on the doors of justice. They cried out for help. They got restraining orders. They pressed charges. Even when their abusers were arrested for assault or for violating orders of pro-

tection, they were back out on bail in the blink of an
eye, angrier and more determined than ever. As far as
we'd come in the eighteen years since I'd first started
fighting on behalf of domestic violence victims, there
were still too many loopholes that a man who was hell-
bent on killing a woman could slip through.

The commission recommended changes in New
York Criminal Procedure Law that would address some
of these loopholes. They included a change in the statutory basis for bail that would include the likelihood of
defendants causing further injury; the mandatory revocation of firearms licenses and the surrender of firearms
when an order of protection is granted; mandatory jail
time for the violation of an order of protection; and the
enforcement of stricter penalties for harassment and
stalking.

We also urged the legislature to expand the definition
of family to reflect accurately the diverse makeup of
modern households. As many as two thirds of domestic
violence victims were not protected by key provisions of
the current law because they didn't fit the state's definition of "family."

Certain protections—mandatory arrest for example—extended only to persons related by blood or marriage, former spouses, and unmarried persons with a
child in common. This narrow definition of family was
preposterous, given the reality of what was occurring in
our communities. The statute could only be inclusive if
it included cohabiting couples, same-sex couples, and

dating couples. To this day, New York State's domestic violence laws don't fully cover unmarried couples living together. To date, only three of the commission's recommendations have been enacted in law. These are: the creation of a separate crime of stalking; the ability to prosecute violations of orders of protection that were issued in other states; and a provision allowing for the suspension or revocation of a firearms license and the surrender of firearms by the subject of an order of protection when divorce, separation, or other disillusion is sought.

One day, while we were still in the process of gathering testimony for the report, I took a drive to Bedford Hills Correctional Facility to talk with an inmate named Linda White. Linda was serving a sentence of seventeen years to life for fatally shooting her thirty-two-year-old boyfriend, John Strouble. When she testified at her trial in 1990 Linda told the jury of her nightmarish existence at the hands of Strouble. She told them about the beatings and jealous rages she suffered when Strouble was high on drugs. She told them of his repeated threats to kill her. She told them about the time he took a handgun, fired it out the window, then put it to her head and pulled the trigger. "Then I went to the bathroom all over myself," she said.

Linda also described how she changed the locks in her home and tried to get help. In desperation, she had gone to Family Court to request an order of protection. She was told, "We can't do anything for you because you're not married to him and you don't have a child in common." So she came back again and lied, saying she was married. Linda got the order of protection, but Strouble tore it up and threw it in her face. Ironically, the fact that she lied would later be used against her by the prosecution at her trial.

Having lost hope that the system would protect her, Linda took the law into her own hands. One night while Strouble was sitting with his back to her, Linda fired four shots into his head. Her story was familiar to anyone who worked on domestic violence cases. Nonetheless, the jury accepted the prosecution's argument that she killed her lover because he threatened to leave her.

The day I met with Linda at the Bedford Hills Correctional Facility I sensed right away that she was a good woman. Certainly, she had killed a man; there was no question about that. But Linda's brown eyes were clear and warm. I believed her story and my heart went out to her. She was not unlike so many other victims who felt abandoned by a system that neither included nor protected them. Linda had tried to abide by society's rules in order to ensure her safety, but society failed to keep its end of the bargain. Renee Linton had also followed the rules, keeping faith with the system whose foremost obligation is to protect its citizens. What good had that done her? The system had failed to protect Linda, and she became a criminal. Since no one listened, she made a desperate choice. My responsibility was to assure that desperate women didn't have to make that choice.

Several years after I visited Linda in prison someone listened. On Christmas Eve, 2002, Governor Pataki granted clemency to Linda White. She had served thirteen years, and she was fifty-five years old.

A few months after her release I received a letter from Linda. She was living near her brother in upstate New York, and she wrote that local domestic violence groups had helped her find an apartment and a job. She thanked me for my support, adding, "It feels so good to be free."

CHAPTER 4

Suffer the Children

The single greatest factor in determining the possibility of criminal behavior on the part of teenagers is not teen pregnancy, drug use, or school truancy. It is whether the teenagers themselves have been the victims of violent crime in or outside their homes.

Violence begets violence. It tears through families and communities like a tornado, a funnel of destruction that expands as it moves. Being abused or neglected as a child increases the likelihood of juvenile arrest by 59 percent, adult arrest by 28 percent, and involvement in violent crime by 30 percent.

It's not an easy thing to swallow—that the seeds of future violence are being planted every day in the minds and hearts of innocents. We have to face it so we can stop it. When I say that a major priority of my office is to support the victims of crime, that is not just an emotional statement, it is a strategic statement. If we have any hope of curtailing future tragedies, we have to begin to identify and attack the circumstances that continue the cycle of violence.

When kids are victimized and abused they will try to protect themselves any way that they can. They will depersonalize their experience. Later, they may suffer flashbacks, become depressed, and show aggression. They may themselves become violent toward others. The cycle will continue. If we ignore the victims of abuse, we are ensuring that the seeds of future criminal conduct have been permanently planted.

Every so often a case comes along that jolts the public into brief consciousness about the brutality toward children that goes on behind closed doors. The public registers shock and outrage. The politicians rush to address the crisis anew. Sometimes these cases are catalysts for change, and that's a good thing; but they represent only a fraction of the cases. The others go unnoticed.

It is especially crucial that those of us who work in law enforcement, the courts, and social services don't become desensitized—that we hold on to our outrage and sense of urgency. For me that has meant keeping the faces of individual children burned into my memory. One of those unforgettable faces belongs to Daniel C.*—not as he is today at age thirty-two, but as he was in 1979, when he was only a nine-year-old boy. Daniel made a big difference in my life.

One day I received an anonymous call at the Domestic Violence Unit. A man's voice, pitched low, gave an address in Yonkers. He said there was a little boy in trouble there. Send police, he told me urgently, then he hung up before I could ask for further details. I called the local police, only to learn that they had also received an anonymous call from a woman about the same situation. Two police officers had been dispatched to the apartment.

The officers were met at the door by a woman who identified herself as Julia Kokinakis. She was eight months pregnant and holding a child who appeared to be about one year old. The officers explained that they were responding to a complaint about a child in trouble. Julia stared at them blankly.

The officers tried to peer behind her into the apartment. "How many children do you have?" one of them asked.

"One," she answered, nodding toward the baby in her arms. "And one on the way."

At that moment, the officers heard a sharp scraping

*Not his real name.

sound and what they thought was a cry coming from behind a closed door. That was all the proof of imminent danger they needed. They entered the apartment and pushed through the door, then stopped short, gasping, as the foul odor of urine and feces hit them. In a corner of the room was a naked boy. He appeared to be five or six years old—filthy, horribly malnourished, completely skin and bones. He was tied to a radiator with the cord from a venetian blind. His matted, unwashed hair was long and stringy, his emaciated body covered with bruises and cuts, his hands swollen black-and-blue from the pinch of the tight cord.

Police officers are accustomed to being exposed to gruesome accident scenes and the terrible aftermath of violence. It is the nature of their work. But they had never seen anything like this. They had to fight to control their emotions as they gently untied the boy from the radiator and wrapped him in a warm blanket. Shocked and unable to comprehend, one of the officers turned to Julia and simply asked, "Why? Why have you done this?"

Her face hardened as she spoke of her son from a previous marriage. "He's a bad boy," she said. "He's always trying to hurt my baby."

Daniel was eventually determined to be nine years old, but the police officers could be excused for misjudging his age. When he arrived at the hospital he was in critical condition. He weighed only forty-eight pounds.

At the hospital I perused Daniel's medical records before going in to see him. The list of his injuries was long: excoriation marks on his wrists where he'd been tied to the radiator, bruises on his head where he'd been struck with a shoe, bruises around his eyes. New scars. Old scars. Starvation. Dehydration. Renal damage. From his dehydrated, malnourished state and the damage to his kidneys and other organs, doctors estimated that he hadn't eaten in at least the last eleven days.

Daniel's tiny body was swallowed up by his bed. An IV dripped nourishment into his veins. He was awake though, and amazingly talkative. He was a highly intelligent little boy. He informed me with some pride that he was nine years old. No, he said, he had never been to school. She wouldn't let him. No, he didn't play outside. She wouldn't let him. We later learned from neighbors that they hadn't even known Julia had a son.

As he spoke, I began to notice that Daniel never referred to Julia as "Mom," or said "my mother." Just "she," or "Julia."

I told him, "I'm going to be your lawyer, Daniel. Do you know what that means?" He shook his head no.

"It means I'm going to protect you . . . make sure you're not hurt again. We'll talk more when you're feeling better. Okay?"

"Okay," he said weakly. There was a hint of a shy smile. I touched his cheek gently, then left the room and went back to work.

I made the decision not to arrest Julia Kokinakis that day. It sounds incredible now, and it didn't seem right then, but I had few options. At that time it was unusual to charge a mother with a felony in New York if she abused or neglected her child. Although the laws had changed regarding domestic violence between adults, similar protections did not yet extend to children. Cases were primarily referred to Family Court and Child Protective Services. Again, the goal was to keep families together. The district attorney's office rarely got involved. The thinking was that having a child testify against his mother would be bad for their relationship once they were reunited. For this reason, I had to proceed carefully.

There wasn't an immediate cry for Julia to be arrested. In fact, the attitude reflected in the media and in our office was quite sympathetic. There was a tremendous amount of pressure not to arrest a woman who was eight months pregnant. Although Daniel and his baby sister were taken away, Julia slept in her own bed—and would do so until the birth of her third child.

I knew one thing, though. I was going to do everything in my power to prosecute Julia for the unthinkable crime she had committed against her young son. Once her baby was born, that baby, too, would be taken away, and she was going to trial. There was a wrong to make right.

On my subsequent hospital visits, I was amazed to see how Daniel was thriving. He loved being in the hospital. He especially loved the nurses, who showered him with affection. Unlike many kids who have been abused, Daniel was neither withdrawn nor aggressive. He was friendly and gregarious, savoring the positive attention for the first time in his life.

I was drawn to this little boy, and I was determined to avoid causing him further pain.

When I told Daniel it would soon be time for him to leave the hospital, his face clouded. "I won't go back there," he said fiercely. "I'll run away." His body heaved and he vomited.

I rushed to comfort him. I knew what I had to do to make sure he was safe. He wouldn't be returned to Julia's care. I explained that he would be going to a home where there were other children, and he would be taken care of.

He was not consoled. Tears streaming down his face, he said, "I don't want to go there. I want to go to a real home. They don't have a mother and father there. I want a mother and a father."

I wanted that for Daniel, too, but that was out of my control. What I could do for him, I realized, was serve as a compassionate and determined advocate. In the coming months, after Daniel was sent to a placement facility, I visited him there as often as I could. He had recovered remarkably. He was much stronger physically and emotionally, and I was glad, because it was time for me to have a very difficult conversation with him.

"Remember when we talked about how I was your lawyer?" I asked. He nodded.

"Well, one of my jobs is to make sure Julia never does this to you or anybody again. That means we have to go to court and tell the people there what happened. And I'll be right there with you. Okay?"

"Sure," he said. He didn't seem at all bothered by this.

"Daniel," I said, leaning in close for a confidential question, "what do *you* think should happen to Julia?"

He didn't even hesitate. "She should go to jail," he replied. "What she did was wrong."

His response surprised and impressed me. Typically, a child who has been brutalized believes that the abuse was his fault. He is more likely to be protective of his abuser, especially if it's his mother. In Daniel's case, this reaction should have been even more pronounced, since he had been completely isolated from normal social interactions. But somehow his innate intelligence allowed him to identify Julia as the criminal who should be held accountable for his suffering.

Julia Kokinakis was convicted of Unlawful Imprisonment, a felony, and was sentenced to jail. Daniel moved to the south to live with his birth father, a good man who took excellent care of him. Daniel kept in touch with me. In the coming years, every so often my secretary would buzz me over the intercom, happily announcing, "It's Daniel. He wants to talk to his lawyer." He always thought of me that way, and I was always delighted to hear his voice.

He called me when he graduated from high school,

then college, where he studied to become a social worker. I was so proud of him.

Daniel beat the odds. He made it out. Most abused children aren't so lucky.

Kids have historically been treated as inconsequential. It should be just the opposite. Who deserves more protection than a vulnerable child? But justice can be blind, even when the consequences are devastating. The first time I tried to prosecute a man for sexually abusing his five-year-old nephew over a period of a year, the case never made it out of the grand jury. The perverted uncle was free to go and abuse other children, and we couldn't do a thing about it. Why? At the time New York had an archaic notion, codified in the penal law, which required a child's testimony concerning sexual abuse to be corroborated—in other words, someone else had to witness the sexual abuse—in order for it to result in a conviction. It was simple. Children's statements held no weight in a court of law. They were deemed inherently unbelievable. The thinking was that children were prone to fantasy. Kids were open to suggestion. Kids were brought into courtrooms by prosecutors and forced to say things against innocent people that weren't true.

If a child claimed to have been a victim of sexual abuse, one of three things was needed to back up the story. The abuser had to admit guilt, which was highly unlikely. There had to be a third-party eyewitness, which was almost inconceivable. Or there had to be compelling medical testimony, which happened sometimes, but not always.

By its very nature, sexual abuse of children happens in secret. Typically, it is carried out by trusted family members, friends of the family, or figures of authority in a child's life. The very idea that there would be eyewitnesses who were not themselves involved stretches the limits of one's imagination. Although sexual abuse is, by its nature, such an egregious violation, there are often no scars or abrasions—at least none for which a wily defense attorney couldn't find other reasons.

Think of how much power this law gave to the abusers. They really were in control. They could do anything they wanted to a child, and nothing would happen to them. I had many, many cases in which children were told by their sexual abusers, "Nobody will believe you." This was the mantra of the pedophile.

Then along came a case for which there was an eyewitness. In 1984 I brought a man named John Hickey to trial. Hickey and his girlfriend, Joan Moore, had sexually abused two young children while Moore baby-sat for them. Moore agreed to testify against Hickey in exchange for five years probation, to be served in a psychiatric center. Perhaps our plea-bargained arrangement with Moore was comparable to making a deal with the devil, but we needed the corroboration. It was the law. And it was very clear that Moore, who was mentally ill, was tangled in a web of Hickey's creation. She was not driven to sexually abuse children, and she sobbed with shame and confusion when she spoke of what had happened that day.

On the afternoon of December 20, 1982, eight-year-old Jimmy* and seven-year-old Judy* were picked up from school by a family friend. The children's foster mother was out of town attending a wedding. Joan Moore, who knew the children, asked their baby-sitter if she could take them to her apartment, which was located in the same building, to have something to eat. Moore took the children to her apartment where John Hickey met them at the door stark naked.

Once inside, the children were ordered to take off their clothes. Hickey and Moore raped and sodomized both children. At one point, a large carving knife and fork were brought from the kitchen and were used on the children as sex toys. Though the instruments did no physical damage, they were enough to terrify the children into silence. When Hickey and Moore were through with them, and the children were allowed to put on their clothes, John Hickey threatened them, saying if they told anyone they would be killed. Hickey and Moore then had intercourse with each other as the terrified children crept out of the room.

When the children were finally taken to Moore's mother's apartment, they hid under the bed, terrified

*Not their real names.

that Hickey would come after them and kill them that day. Joan Moore's mother didn't understand and told the kids to stop playing around. They tried to explain what they were so afraid of, but no one believed them.

Still, their foster mother couldn't help noticing a startling change in the children when she returned from the wedding. They were so quiet and listless, not at all normal for these spirited kids, especially the week before Christmas. The truth came out when Joan Moore confided to her mother, and then the children's foster mother was told.

The children's foster family was devastated. They had tried to give these once-abandoned kids a normal life. Now they feared that this new horror would permanently traumatize them.

The trial of John Hickey did not take place for another year and a half. That's typical of the sluggish process of our overburdened justice system. By then, Jimmy was nine and a half and Judy was eight and a half. They would be testifying at trial and we would be using anatomically correct dolls to help them demonstrate what had happened to them.

The pretrial hearings were long and bitterly divisive. Hickey's attorney strenuously objected to the use of the dolls. He appealed to the judge that if the children were old enough to testify truthfully, then they could explain what had happened in their own words. Using dolls was play-acting with the prosecutor, he argued.

The judge rightly denied the motion. The anatomically correct dolls, which were innocuous Raggedy Ann–style, were an important tool in gaining accurate testimony from small children. They didn't know the terminology for the crimes committed against them. They didn't know how to talk about sodomy, about penises and vaginas. They could use the dolls to show what they couldn't find the words for.

An important consideration when young children are testifying is whether or not they are capable of understanding the meaning of the oath. Essentially, the court must determine that a child witness is able to appreciate the difference between truth and falsehood. Kids lie just as adults lie. Most of them, just like adults, have the wherewithal to know when they're doing it.

When Judy took the stand, the judge spent a few minutes making sure she understood the importance of telling the truth. He asked her if she knew what had happened to Pinocchio when he told a lie, and Judy giggled nervously and said, "His nose grew long." I thought this was an odd example, since it was in the realm of fantasy, and no one was suggesting that Judy's nose would grow if she lied on the stand. She got it right when the judge asked, "Do you know what happens if somebody tells a lie?"

Judy replied soberly, "They get punished from my mother and from God."

Judy and Jimmy were very brave and resolute on the stand. They withstood hours of testimony and cross-examination, patiently demonstrating every act that had been forced upon them, using the dolls. Although Joan Moore testified for the prosecution and confirmed the children's story, the defense was based almost entirely on a case of mistaken identity—that the children were confused, that I prodded them to point the finger at John Hickey.

But you could hear in their testimony that they were extremely clear. The children were powerful and convincing. As I told the jury in my closing argument, "There is a passage in the Bible: 'Out of the mouths of babes hast thou ordained strength.' When you heard those children—when those children took those dolls, and when they showed you how the sexual acts were perpetrated upon them—didn't that ring true to you?"

It did. The jury returned a verdict of guilty on all counts.

In sentencing Hickey to twenty-five to seventy-five years in prison, the judge angrily rebuked him. "You engaged in a cruel, vicious, and merciless exercise in terror for your own gratification, both psychological and sexual . . . you have failed to exhibit even the slightest compassion for the fate of your innocent victims, whom you used and abused for your perverse pleasure and who must now face each and every day of their lives haunted by nightmares."

It was a premonition that was sadly true. We knew very little about how to take care of the victims of these crimes. There was no support system in place, and although we recommended counseling, it didn't always happen—either because families couldn't afford it, or because they wanted to forget the past. Parents and relatives were often more concerned about putting the horrible incidents behind them—attempting to restore a normalcy that was no longer truly possible.

Eight years after John Hickey's trial, as a County Court Judge, I looked out into the courtroom one day and the hairs on the back of my neck stood on end as if I'd been jolted by a bolt of lightning. I was looking into a pair of pretty blue eyes set in a cherubic face that I would never forget. It was Judy. She was sixteen now, and she was in trouble.

She had tried to commit suicide. Her brother, Jimmy, I learned, was involved in male prostitution. We expected these young children, their innocence shattered so long ago, to heal on their own, to make all the right choices by themselves.

What had we done? In essence, we had sentenced them as well. By failing to treat them as victims in need of continued therapy and help we had thrown them away. Should we have been surprised to find them living their broken lives among the outcasts of society?

The cycle of violence continues. Michael Linton, Jr., who witnessed his father shoot his mother in 1987, when he was ten years old, was prosecuted by my office in 1999 for shooting a man five times. He is currently serving twenty years in prison.

. . .

We can't continue to live with the fiction that once we identify the abusers of kids like Judy and Jimmy and convict them, the children will be able to go on with their lives and be just fine. Little children can't be normal under these circumstances. Nobody could. They need to be nurtured and counseled until their sense of safety has been restored and they are well.

Our society is so intent on rehabilitating the criminal element. We have a whole department of probation to monitor a defendant's behavior. We make sure that they enter some form of therapy, whether drug treatment, alcohol treatment, or anger management. We make sure that they go to their meetings. We have a whole section in the penal law that allows us to bring them back to court to make sure they're doing the right thing and keeping their noses clean.

Why aren't we focusing on the victim, rehabilitating the person on whom the criminal chose to prey? Our obligation is to give them at least as much support as we do the criminal.

How can we go about doing so? I'd propose this: When a child is physically or sexually abused, or harmed in some other life-shattering way, we should require that the child be monitored and participate in some therapy. That therapy should involve group support as well—sessions with other kids who have been similarly abused—because the natural inclination is to think it's your fault, that you're the only one to whom this has ever happened.

Look at what happened to Jimmy. It's a classic case.

Obviously, no one was monitoring this kid. He had un-resolved emotions and confusion about sex. He could have been saved if we'd had a system in place to track and help him, to assess the pitfalls he would face when he started to deal with his own sexuality. If you are raped as a child, what is going to happen to you when you come of age and become a sexual being yourself? Your only context for a sexual relationship is violence and hu-miliation. We have to intervene to change that damaged interior sexual model so these kids can shed their fright-ening pasts and try to lead normal lives.

The good news is that it *is* possible to recover. We need to keep that vision of hope in front of us, so that we don't despair and decide it is pointless even to try saving the children damaged by unspeakable abuse. Connie Rogers* symbolizes that hope for me.

George Rogers* will rot in jail for what he did to his family. He was considered an upstanding citizen, highly regarded by all in the community, but behind closed doors he made his home a torture chamber, inflicting rape, drugs, beatings, and sadistic games that culminated in murder.

In 1982, George Rogers, who owned a successful jewelry store in Manhattan, was living in New Rochelle with his second wife, Mary,* who was thirty. They had

*Not their real names.

three small children, ages two, three, and five. Also living in the household were George's two children from his first marriage—Connie, fourteen, and John,* twelve.

The evening of December 23 began in what had become a typical scenario in this house of horrors. When Mary served dinner, George exploded in a rage. Throwing his plate on the floor, he screamed, "This is fucking shit. How dare you serve me this garbage?"

Throughout the night, the children tried to stay out of sight in their rooms, but they could hear their father's voice through the walls, threatening, "I'm going to keep hitting you, you fucking bitch, until you start bleeding."

At some point, George called out to Connie, and she entered the bedroom nervously. Mary was lying in bed. Her father told her that Mary was feeling ill and instructed her to bring a glass of milk from the kitchen. Connie did as she was told, then went back to bed. Shortly, her father called her again, and she returned to the bedroom. "Something is very wrong," George told her, and ordered her to get her brother.

As Mary lay dead, Connie vacuumed up white powder and picked up broken bottles, while John disposed of a bloody towel. After instructing the children to tell anyone who asked that they were a happy family, George finally called the police. Mary had been dead five hours, her body already stiff. George's story was that his wife was a cocaine abuser who had committed sui-

*Not their real names.

cide. In truth, George had forced Mary to drink the glass of milk Connie had brought, laced with enough cocaine to kill a horse. The medical examiner ruled that Mary had died of acute cocaine poisoning, but the manner of her death was stated as unknown.

Life went on in George Rogers's household, and the horror continued, only worse for Connie. Almost immediately after Mary's death, her father informed Connie that she would be taking her stepmother's place—in every way. He initiated his fourteen-year-old daughter into his brutal sex rituals, which involved severe beatings, followed by sodomy and forced intercourse. He made her dress in Mary's clothes and ordered the children to call her "Mommy." He kept her out of school for days and weeks at a time. On occasion, he would order Connie to come to his jewelry store, where he would rape her in the storage room. When she got pregnant in September 1983, George took Connie for an abortion, and told the doctor she was eighteen and impregnated by her boyfriend.

The terror was finally suspended in April 1984, when George was arrested, on federal charges of running a cocaine ring from his jewelry store. Even in prison, he tried to maintain his strict hold, writing Connie voluminous letters and insisting that she reply in kind. It took Connie another year to face what had happened to her and to summon the courage to come forward.

I met Connie in May 1985, when her case was assigned to the Domestic Violence/Child Abuse Unit. I was impressed by how smart and resourceful she was. I presented the case to the grand jury, who voted to indict George Rogers on twenty-five counts of Forcible Sodomy and Rape. I took the case to trial in January 1987.

Through it all, Connie was stalwart and determined. The jury found her credible. When her father was convicted on all counts and sentenced to twenty-five years, I made sure Connie knew that she had done the right thing. She had a right to go on without being haunted every day of her life by the memories.

I was touched by Connie. The fact that she carried on in spite of the trauma she had experienced was a testament to her strength of character. She would need to call on that strength one more time.

During our conversations, Connie had told me about the night Mary died, and the prior abuse and threats she had experienced. The pattern of domestic violence leading to homicide was unmistakable. I began to look into Mary's death. I was struck by the accounts of all who knew her that she was a happy woman who loved and cared for three children, and who had never touched cocaine. The night she died, she was wrapping Christmas presents for the children and wearing a blinking reindeer pin, in the spirit of the season. It didn't appear to be the conduct of someone contemplating suicide.

For me, the clincher was looking at the autopsy photos. I noticed something that convinced me this woman had not committed suicide. It was the kind of detail a man wouldn't necessarily see, but a woman would. Mary was impeccable. Her eyebrows were perfectly tweezed. Her nails were freshly painted with bright red polish. I thought to myself, a woman so depressed that she's planning to commit suicide doesn't tweeze her eyebrows, get a manicure, and prepare to celebrate a holiday she had no intention of living to see. It was the false note that led to the unraveling of all the other lies.

Eventually, I would take George Rogers back to trial for Mary's murder. In the course of my investigation, I learned from George's first wife that he had threatened her, too, once saying that he could have her killed as he'd had other people killed. This was a key admission by the defendant, but the jury never heard it. It was barred as a confidential husband-wife communication, even though it involved a husband's threat to kill his wife. Nonetheless, I secured a Second-Degree Murder conviction. His sentence of twenty-five years to life would be added to the twenty-five years he was already serving for Connie's rape.

What would become of Connie, who now faced the task of erasing those long nights and days of terror, pain, and degradation? I made a commitment to stay close to Connie, who went back to live with her mother. I wrote a letter of recommendation when she applied to college, and kept in touch with her. She had decided to become a lawyer, to devote her life to justice. It was a fitting ideal, and I believe it furthered her healing. Years later, when she graduated from law school and passed the bar she came to work in my office as an assistant district attorney. I was honored to have her. She would be the best advocate any victim could have, because she'd been there, and now she was a bright, shining example of hope.

CHAPTER 5

Behind Closed Doors

In the early 1980s, when I was prosecuting sexual deviants like John Hickey, I couldn't have imagined how enormous the world of pedophilia was, or how determined these men were—for they were almost always men—to have sex with our children. I am wiser now, and even more determined. We must spare no effort in putting them away.

Soon after I became district attorney in 1994, I encountered an entirely new twist on the sick old theme. The Internet, blossoming like a noxious weed, has brought the pedophiles right into our kids' bedrooms. No matter how many parental controls we set up, no matter how many firewalls we build, the worst perverts imaginable have found a means to gain easy access to our children. They lurk in teen chat rooms, invisible and un-detected. For Internet pedophiles, ensnaring kids is as easy as taking candy from a baby.

Parents are often unaware of the fact that, behind the closed doors of bedrooms and dens, their kids are im-mersed in a dark world—not necessarily because the kids seek it out, but because the predators stalk them electronically. I once asked a group of middle school students, "How many of you have gone on-line at night when your parents are sleeping and think you are asleep?" More than half of them raised their hands.

These twelve- to fourteen-year-olds are prime targets for the worst kind of scum. When they log on to the In-ternet, they crack open the door that allows predators to slip into their normally safe homes. If parents knew what was going on, they wouldn't be able to sleep.

Alan Paul Barlow was one of these devious electronic stalkers. In 1994 the fifty-one-year-old Seattle postal worker began exchanging e-mails with a fourteen-year-old girl in Westchester County he had "met" in an In-ternet chat room. Initially, he posed as a teenager. The girl was naive, and the e-mails intrigued her. She didn't tell her mother. She didn't tell her friends. It was her se-cret, and it made her feel grown up when Barlow wrote about all the things his "Oscar" would like to do with her "Love Bunny." A typical message from Barlow read:

I'm feeling really horny—I think Oscar is making a "statement." We both want you very much. I'm

thinking about you, & he's thinking about Love
Bunny & tingling like mad.

After six months, Barlow admitted his true age and
told the girl he wanted to meet her and suggested that
he fly to the East Coast for a visit. She agreed. Barlow
flew to New York, booked a motel room, and called the
girl. Telling her mother that she was taking her eight-
year-old brother to the school playground, she left to
meet Barlow with her brother in tow. The children
spent some time at the school with Barlow, and he took
pictures of them. When the boy said he was thirsty, Barlow drove them to a nearby drugstore to get a drink.

Things could have gone very badly at that point but
for a remarkable stroke of luck. The children's mother
happened to be coming out of the drugstore when she
spotted them standing with a strange man. She took
them home, and the girl told her everything. Barlow
was later arrested at his motel.

Investigators soon discovered that Barlow had been
e-mailing teenagers in several states. He had also been
using regular mail to send samples of his semen to one
girl and pictures of his penis to others.

Barlow was a hard-core predator. He would never
stop unless we locked him up, but we had few options.
It wasn't a felony to send pornographic e-mails, even to
minors. Since Barlow had been caught before he sexually
abused the girl, the most we could charge him with was
Endangering the Welfare of a Minor, a misdemeanor.

But this kind of conduct is never a one-time thing. Pedophiles like Barlow are notorious recidivists. If we
could get the word of his latest crime out to the public,
I was convinced that more victims would come forward.

We began an intensive investigation. We contacted
out-of-state law enforcement agencies and notified the
news media. The unique facts of the crime grabbed the
attention of news outlets, and Barlow became a national
story. One parent in Montana heard a radio broadcast
about the arrest and notified police. Barlow had been
engaged in similar activities with the man's daughter.
Our investigation also led us to victims in Minnesota,
New Jersey, and Washington State.

Before Barlow made bail on our case, Washington
State officials were able to compile enough evidence to
charge him with the rape of a minor. As he stepped off
the plane in Seattle, he was arrested and handcuffed. Ultimately, he was convicted of the rape and sent to prison.

I knew we had to figure out a way to stop criminals
like Barlow for good, but it wasn't going to be easy. The
Internet existed on the frontier of cyberspace, and we had
only just begun to establish the legal ground rules for this
new territory. There was no statute that specifically covered the behavior of determined high-tech pedophiles
like Barlow, because lawmakers hadn't imagined it could
happen. In this instance, the predators had a real head-
start on the law.

The Barlow case galvanized some attention, but not

enough to make a lasting public impression. If these same communications had occurred on public streets, in stores, or in schoolyards, people would be up in arms. When it happened in their own homes, in their children's bedrooms, it received little notice and no appropriate criminal punishment under our laws.

I launched a crusade for new laws and began lobbying for a change in New York's penal law to make it a felony to engage in indecent communication with a minor over the Internet. Many people, including Governor George Pataki, supported this effort. There was also strong resistance. Some legislators worried that the proposed law would be unconstitutional, violating First Amendment rights. I was completely unmoved, even disgusted by this argument. Since when was the First Amendment intended to protect dirty middle-aged men who spew filth at our children? Sometimes our legislators need to be reminded that they are not dealing in abstractions. The pedophiles can get to their children, too.

I was absolutely clear about this. Our constitutional principles meant nothing if they weren't grounded in our fundamental values. A civilized society could not afford to be ambivalent about the sexual exploitation and abuse of its children.

Finally, in 1996 the New York State Legislature passed a law that made it a felony for an adult to use the Internet to communicate with a minor in a sexually explicit manner and to induce a minor into sexual activity.

This law, the first of its kind in the nation, allowed us to begin hunting down the perverts in the vast terrain of the World Wide Web.

I began an Internet-pedophile sting operation in the summer of 1999, running it out of the White Plains, New York, courthouse where my offices are located. It's a bare-bones operation run by Pat Storino, an experienced criminal investigator. Using laptop computers, Pat and his team drift in and out of chat rooms posing as young girls or young boys. It's tedious work, requiring the utmost skill and patience. My investigators have to inhabit the minds and ape the lingo of teenagers and pedophiles alike. When they do get a nibble, they have to proceed very carefully. The investigators never lead. They carefully follow. When and if the target suggests a "meet," they agree. The pedophile arrives on the scene and is met by an officer with a badge and a gun, not by his imagined child correspondent.

We are scrupulous about the way we conduct our stings, since the first thing these guys do when they get caught is cry "Entrapment!" We have no desire to entrap; it destroys the legal underpinnings of any case we may bring. Legally, entrapment is defined as a law enforcement officer actively inducing or encouraging someone to commit a crime, when that person is not otherwise predisposed to do so. That is not the case here.

Our investigators do not initiate the sexual conversations. They do not initiate the meetings.

In their on-line chats, they always make it crystal clear that they are minors. Usually, they just go on-line and wait. Sometimes, within moments of entering a teen chat room our investigator will get hit on. He doesn't have to make overtures. He doesn't have to make believe he wants sex, or that he's sexually curious, or that he's looking for a date. An investigator will sign on, say he's a fourteen-year-old boy living in White Plains, New York, and before long someone will start communicating with him, asking sexually explicit questions.

It's chilling. The majority of people coming to call in these chat rooms are middle-aged, middle income, fairly well-educated men. By day, they're respected, established members of the community with jobs in business, education, and government. The Internet gives their sick passions a perfectly anonymous cover.

The sting operation has been successful, since we are careful to operate strictly within the law. We get results. To date, we have made seventy-two arrests, with sixty-five convictions and seven cases pending. We have a 100-percent conviction rate, and none of the convictions have been overturned on appeal. One advantage of the Internet is that it gives us an impeccable record of the crime. By the time the cases are charged, they're solid. Several other law enforcement agencies in New York and beyond have sought our help in developing similar operations.

Even so, the Internet sting operation remains controversial. There are still plenty of skeptics around who simply cannot believe that the Internet poses such a risk to our children. They think perverts are guys in trench coats hanging around outside elementary schools, lurking in public parks, or patrolling video arcades. But cyberspace has created a vast new world of access, allowing predators to cast a wide net. They are not just on the streets, they are now in our homes.

They are not easily deterred. Some of these pedophiles are so brazen that they continue their contact with children even after they are caught. One such deviant, convicted in a neighboring county for sodomizing a minor, was out on bail awaiting sentence. He used this time to troll the Internet, looking for new victims. Fortunately, he ended up targeting our undercover, and within two minutes sent a sexually explicit communication. He drove sixty miles to Westchester to meet with his prey and was placed under arrest. He is now in state prison for both crimes.

Yet another stellar citizen, a lawyer and Harvard graduate, was convicted by my office of an Internet sex crime. He continued to prowl the Internet in violation of his probation, and we stung him again. Now he's behind bars.

These cases aren't isolated. In fact, in more than one out of five of the arrests we've made to date, we've uncovered additional evidence that the defendants have actually abused children or trafficked in child pornography.

Internet predators are so determined to satisfy their own needs that they will take extraordinary risks. Our stings have received a lot of publicity, and the pedophiles are aware that we're out there. They know they're taking a chance. They'll write, "You aren't from Pirro's office, are you?" and our investigator, posing as a teenager, will write back, "No." The pedophile, desperate to believe it, accepts the investigator's denial as truth. Unrelenting, he continues his pursuit.

With tens of millions of computers connected to the Internet, how many more Alan Paul Barlows are out there in the dark, preying on our children from the comfort of their homes? We must update our laws to address this high-tech form of child abuse.

In May 2001 we arrested a Connecticut priest after he engaged in sexually explicit on-line conversations with one of our investigators who was posing as a fourteen-year-old boy. This was a particularly sad case. Father John Castaldo, forty-three, was the spiritual director at a Catholic high school in Stamford, Connecticut. He was the person to whom other priests and teachers sent young boys who felt the urge to masturbate—behavior the Church deemed sinful. In 2001 he was looking for prey on the Internet.

During the on-line chat with our investigator, Father Castaldo was very explicit about the sexual acts he wanted to engage in—including mutual masturbation while on-line and on the phone, and oral sex. He was also extremely cautious, asking numerous questions about the fictitious youth to ascertain that he was a real teenager. At one point he wrote, "I've got a lot to lose." Indeed, he did, but he was still willing to risk it.

The arrest of Father Castaldo was an ominous precursor to the massive explosion of pedophilia cases that would soon rock the Catholic Church to its very foundation and cause many law enforcement officials to reassess their deferential, hands-off policies with the Church.

In January 2002 the *Boston Globe* published a story about John Geoghan, a pedophile priest who had been protected by the Boston archdiocese for many years. *Globe* reporters learned that a conspiracy to cover up the actions of pedophile clergy infused Church hierarchy and went as high as Boston's own Cardinal Bernard Law, one of the most influential Catholic officials in the United States. Geoghan's case was particularly shocking because his actions had been so unrelenting, and he had remained unrepentant over the years. When individual complaints became too loud to ignore, his superiors reassigned Geoghan to a new parish, where he could start over. Nearly two hundred victims came forward claiming that Geoghan had raped or fondled them as children.

The *Globe*'s story opened a vast floodgate of repressed private pain, as hundreds of victims across the nation came forward with their own horrific stories of being

sodomized and raped by priests. The public was stunned
to learn that the Church hid the truth from its trusting
congregations.

I wanted to make sure that the New York Archdiocese cooperated fully with law enforcement, and I was
concerned when Church authorities took a confronta-
tional approach to the issue.

Many DAs in the Archdiocese wanted immediate access to records of sexual-abuse allegations, but the Archdiocese announced that it would review the allegations
and pass on only those they believed to be legitimate.

This was absolutely unacceptable. A religious institution that had managed to cover up sexual-abuse allegations for decades was in no position to make such
crucial judgments. All reports of allegations were to be
passed on to us immediately. Law enforcement, not the
Church, would decide which incidents were worthy of
prosecution.

The Archdiocese had good reason to expect a certain
level of deference from New York authorities. It had always straddled the Church-state line in its relationships
with political and civic leaders. It wielded enormous
power and influence. When the Archdiocese asked authorities to back off, there was a general sentiment that
such a request was reasonable.

I disagreed. I wanted those records.

Soon I began receiving calls from friends and colleagues in Church and government circles. The pressure

was applied gently, but the point was unmistakable. These were people who had supported me politically. They urged me to ease up. The Church deserved some consideration, especially from one of its own.

I am a practicing Catholic, raised in the Church, educated in Catholic schools. My faith is an important part of my identity, and it informs my moral code. If anything, the cover-up by Catholic officials is all the more egregious because they are men of God. Their calling is to shepherd the faithful, not deliver them to the wolves.

It was time to act. In April 2002, I arranged a meeting in my office. Present were seven other DAs whose jurisdictions fell within the New York Archdiocese and five lawyers representing the Archdiocese.

"I'm a devout Catholic," I told the twelve men at the outset. "I understand my moral obligation, and I know my legal obligation. They are the same." Then I told the Church lawyers that my fellow prosecutors and I needed access to their records—all of them. "We, not you, will determine whether there is sufficient evidence to prosecute," I said.

The lawyers replied that the Archdiocese was committed to learning the truth about every allegation of sexual abuse. In fact, it was prepared to establish a commission, composed of the most well-respected members of the community, to study the charges and determine which were legitimate.

I appreciated their intentions, but this would not be acceptable. "With all due respect," I said, "my colleagues and I have extensive experience in these matters. There is no doubt that your commission members would be well-meaning, but they wouldn't have the expertise to judge the merits of such accusations. This is no longer a concern of the Church. This is a question of law enforcement."

Ultimately, the Archdiocese agreed to turn over the records.

The issue of secrecy agreements also had to be addressed. In the past, when victims came forward and complained to Church officials, they were sometimes paid cash settlements in exchange for their silence. Although they were not binding in criminal prosecutions, sealed secrecy agreements discouraged victims from coming forward. In my opinion, such agreements should be banned when children are involved. We wanted the Archdiocese officially to release people from those agreements as a way of encouraging victims to come forward. A week after our meeting, the Archdiocese announced that, "in a spirit of cooperation," all secrecy agreements would be invalid. To its credit, the Archdiocese went on to cooperate fully in the investigations to come.

As our office and others nationwide dealt with the flood of allegations against priests, some dating back twenty years or more, we confronted a major legal roadblock to prosecuting these crimes. The statute of limitations that applies to most crimes was applicable in these cases.

The premise of the statute of limitations is that there

comes a point in time when a case becomes stale and a defendant may be unable to defend himself. We have always balanced the potential of stale evidence with the gravity of the crime. Murder has never had a statute of limitations. Many people—and I am one of them—believe there should be an exemption for the sexual abuse of a child. Because the pain suffered by the victims never goes away, next to murder, no crime is more serious. Child sex offenders are also notorious recidivists. The passage of time does not diminish their criminal desire—nor should it diminish our ability to prosecute them. Furthermore, the delay is usually a direct result of the crime itself.

Our experience with pedophile priests has raised a highly relevant question: Should the defendant benefit from the fact that it was his own conduct that intimidated a victim and made him fearful of coming forward? Why should he profit from his own wrongdoing?

Statutes that give the worst predators a free ride if they can just run out the clock show contempt for the victims. In New York State, almost every crime is subject to a statute of limitations. You can sexually abuse a child, and if he doesn't come forward before he's twenty-three, the crime is wiped off the slate. It never happened.

Since all but a handful of states have statutes of limitation on child sexual abuse, most prosecutors have seen pedophile priests slipping through the fingers of the law, since their crimes were not reported to law enforcement earlier. Advocates of the statutes, who felt it would be wrong to prosecute crimes dating back decades, blamed the victims for not reporting the abuse earlier. Of course they didn't report it. More than 60 percent of all sex crimes are never reported at all. If children are terrified of turning in adults who sexually abuse them, think of the extra pressure involved when their abuser is a priest.

We interviewed many victims now in their twenties and thirties who had finally summoned the courage to come forward. They were consumed with fear—that they wouldn't be believed, that they'd be ostracized, that they'd be blamed. They were full of shame. In every case, the victim carried a heavy burden of self-loathing.

When a child is sexually abused by a person whom everyone reveres, including his parents, do we seriously expect that child to come forward? How can we look him in the face and say, "Sorry, you should have told someone about this sooner. It's too late now."

In some instances courageous children did report the abuse to their parents. When these angry parents confronted the priests' superiors they were assured that the Church would handle the matter. These people were good Catholics, faithful to Mother Church. They were conditioned to trust the clergy. Little did they know that the offending priests were being reassigned to new parishes where they were free to abuse other unsuspecting parents' children.

As a result of actions by the Catholic Church, entire

categories of crime victims were denied access to the criminal justice system. Some parents believed that cases would be reported to law enforcement. Others believed that removal of the offending priest from their parish meant that he would be dismissed from the priesthood, when in fact he was merely transferred to another parish. Some thought that the offender was being punished. All were wrong. No one in the Church was punishing priests; no one was protecting victims.

I'll never forget the mother who told me, "I believed them when they said they would do the right thing. They even thanked us for coming forward. It never occurred to me to call the police. I trusted them that much. Now I have all the other children this man abused on my conscience."

To mislead people so brazenly and to later hide behind a statute of limitations is immoral. Do we as a society really believe that people who commit rape, assault, and sexual abuse of children should be walking our streets because we didn't catch them in time? Does this statute reflect the values and mores of our community? Of course not. And that should be the standard we adhere to, that should be the test.

I created a dedicated hotline to accept calls from potential victims and ran a newspaper ad encouraging victims to come forward. They needed to have confidence that their stories would be heard and fully investigated.

Legislators across the country were also reviewing

laws already on the books about reporting the sexual abuse of children. The cloak of privacy traditionally given to the Catholic Church was being reevaluated. In about twenty states there was no requirement that clergy report such abuse to the authorities. Most states also had exemptions for revelations made inside the sanctuary of a confessional, so, even when priests confessed to their superiors, the admissions were not revealed. Eliminating the confessional exemption was controversial, but at least two states—Texas and New Hampshire—wrote laws that did just that. Many children's advocates believed that when it came to the well-being of minors, there should be no exemptions.

On April 29, 2002, after the New York Archdiocese had turned over its records, I impaneled a special grand jury to investigate those cases. The grand jury met fifteen times, heard testimony from more than twenty witnesses, and reviewed exhibits consisting of thousands of documents. While all of these cases proved to be barred from prosecution by the statute of limitations, the grand jury used the information to make recommendations to the New York legislature. Their recommendations, presented in mid-June, included the elimination of the statute of limitations for child sexual abuse, mandatory reporting by religious institutions, criminal penalties for recklessly allowing an employee with a record of child sexual abuse access to minors, and prohibition of confidentiality agreements in civil suits regarding child sexual abuse. These recommendations are still being reviewed by the state legislature.

The law moves at a leisurely pace, even as our children suffer. As each day passes, more victims fall by the wayside. In 2003, the U.S. Supreme Court ruled that once a statute of limitations expires, it cannot be revived by subsequent legislation. This ruling effectively bars thousands of victims of childhood sexual assault from receiving justice. The time we lose now cannot be recovered.

CHAPTER 6

A Wink and a Nod

In the Harrison High School yearbook he didn't live to see, Robert Viscome was named "Class Partier" and "Most likely to extend the weekend." It was a chilling forecast.

On April 23, 2002, there was an electrical outage at Harrison High School. Classes were suspended, freeing the student body of almost eight hundred to enjoy the late spring day. One of the girls, a sixteen-year-old junior, told friends her parents were out of town, and she invited them to party at her luxurious home, which had a wet bar and a lavishly outfitted game room.

Heading to the party, Robert Viscome and his friend and football teammate, Nicholas Rukaj, stopped at a local deli to buy beer. Viscome went inside while Rukaj waited in the car. The deli had signs posted that read: "No ID—no alcohol. Don't waste your time or mine." The legal drinking age is twenty-one. Although only seventeen, Viscome, who was six feet tall with a full beard, pulled it off. He purchased several six packs of beer and some forty-ounce bottles of malt liquor. Then he drove Rukaj over to the party.

During the next few hours more than two dozen teenagers came in and out of the house, and there was heavy drinking. At some point, an intoxicated Robert Viscome, who may have consumed as many as twelve beers, and Nicholas Rukaj got into a dispute. Viscome made an insulting remark about Rukaj's father, who was doing time in jail for murder. Rukaj's younger brother, Patrick, overheard the remark and shoved Viscome against the wall. When other kids yelled for them to take it outside, they did. Outside, they faced off and Pat Rukaj threw a punch. Viscome's knees buckled, and he fell backward, smacking his head on the flagstone patio.

What happened once Viscome was lying unconscious on the patio was extremely disturbing. Not one of the teenagers made a move to call 911, or a parent, or a neighbor. At that moment, the biggest concern in the group was that Viscome would be found injured and unconscious at this private home where they were drinking. They decided to cover their tracks.

Maybe some of the kids were in shock. Many of them were inebriated. It was unconscionable and shameful. It was disturbing that these kids didn't have moral instincts that cried out for urgent action.

Instead, they thought only of themselves and the trouble they might be in. A group of teens hauled Viscome up and hustled him out to a car. They decided to take him to the nearby United Hospital Medical Center in Port Chester but agreed not to reveal where his injuries had occurred. They told the emergency room physician who examined him that Viscome was injured while wrestling in a local park. A nurse at United Hospital called the Harrison Police and gave a report. A Harrison police officer was dispatched to the park to look for evidence.

Four teenagers were now at the hospital waiting for news of Viscome's condition. For all they knew, their handling of Viscome could have made his condition worse. Fortunately for them, this wasn't the case. According to the Medical Examiner, Viscome's fate was sealed the moment his head hit the flagstone. But his friends didn't know that. They wondered what to tell the authorities when they were asked. Finally, they decided, one by one, to tell the truth.

Slowly, painfully, the details were revealed. From many different accounts came one clear story.

Patrick Rukaj was arrested and charged with assault. Robert Viscome was placed on life support and transferred to the trauma center at Westchester Medical Center in Valhalla. Tests indicated he was in a deep coma. His skull was fractured, and there was a massive bruise on his brain. A week later, as April turned to May, the machines sustaining Robert Viscome's life were disconnected.

The justice system is designed to hold people responsible for acts that our society defines as criminal, but like all systems it is finite and limited. In New York, it's not a crime to lie to a police officer. Nor is it illegal to fail to call 911 when someone is injured. The high school students who passively watched their dying friend, worrying more about the trouble they might encounter than his welfare, could not be prosecuted. As shameful and reprehensible as their conduct was, it was not criminal under the law.

While Patrick Rukaj, the teenager who threw the punch, ultimately pled guilty to assault, the investigation clearly established that he hadn't intended to kill Robert Viscome. Nor was Robert's death a plainly foreseeable result of the punch. Viscome died only because his head had hit the flagstone in a very unusual manner.

Were these flaws in the criminal justice system? Should failing to call for help or lying to the police be crimes? Should inflicting a blow that results in death be regarded as criminal homicide, regardless of a person's intent or the freakishness of the result?

I think so. It is often true that a set of unique facts highlights a deficiency in our system. This was one such case. Perhaps the Viscome incident will serve as a wake-up call on these legal shortfalls, just as it served as a wake-up call on one deadly and pervasive issue: the tragic consequences of underage drinking.

If we knew there was a serial killer in our midst, we'd pull out all the stops to catch him. Everyone in the community would be focused on that goal. You wouldn't hear people saying, "There's nothing we can do."

How is this any different than the murderous epidemic of underage drinking? It moves stealthily through our neighborhoods, collecting young victims when no one is watching. The problem worsens every year, yet most people remain remarkably blasé.

Almost immediately after I became DA in 1994, I was hit hard by the deaths of two teenagers who had been served alcohol illegally at two bars in New Rochelle. Several years later, in December 1999, an Iona college student died of toxic alcohol poisoning during a fraternity hazing. He literally drank himself to death.

The casual manner in which these young people obtained alcohol, and their complete disregard for the dangers of excessive drinking was deeply troubling. Had we placed so much emphasis on waging a "War on Drugs" that we'd ignored the toll alcohol was taking on our youth? Why weren't we waging a "War on Alcohol"?

Alcohol is an "acceptable" drug, present in most homes. It's easy to come by. There is virtually no public discussion about the dangers of drinking. To the contrary, many of our most sacred rituals—from weddings to holidays to sporting events—are associated with alcohol.

A 2002 study released by the National Center on Addiction and Substance Abuse at Columbia University reports that America is experiencing an epidemic of underage drinking that begins in elementary and middle school. According to the study, more than five million high school students admit to binge drinking at least once a month. The report's authors point the finger at parents as "unwitting coconspirators" in this epidemic. Parents view alcohol use by their teens as a rite of passage, rather than as a deadly round of Russian roulette, that they have both a legal and a moral obligation to stop. With a wink and a nod, parents let their kids know that there's no harm in having a couple of beers—all the kids do it. I know this because I've heard parents say it.

Recently, we prosecuted a parent who hosted a sweet sixteen party for her daughter that involved binge drinking. Kids were passed out on the lawn and vomiting in the bushes. When we confronted the mother and asked what on earth she'd been thinking, she said, "I'd rather have them drinking here, where I can supervise them." Some supervision!

Another parent stood at the door of his home passing out cups, for which he collected five dollars from teenage partygoers. There was a keg inside the house. He explained to cops that it was a fund-raiser for the high school trip to Cancun.

In September 2001, in Chappaqua, a wealthy bedroom community in Westchester, parents hosted a party for their seventeen-year-old son's school football team. Not only was alcohol present, but a stripper served as the entertainment. When police, responding to neighbors' complaints of loud noise, arrived at the residence, a group of drunken teenage boys was huddled around a nude young woman, licking whipped cream off her body and inserting objects into her private parts.

Parents who host drinking parties and allow strippers to be hired for the entertainment of children deserve to be prosecuted. Yet, every time one of these situations arises, people rush to their defense. We hear all about what good families these are, how they meant no harm, how the kids were good kids, how they were just letting off steam. It's appalling. When student athletes, especially football players, are involved, the defenses are even louder. There is a belief within the culture of football, even at the high school level, that the players are entitled to drink after a tough season. They're entitled to lick whipped cream off a stripper. Their testosterone is high.

Last year, a high school football team held a drinking party to celebrate the start of the season. During the party, a star player was injured when he slammed his arm through a plate-glass window. The school's football coach refused to speak with the assistant district attorney I put on the case. What kind of message does that send?

Don't tell me boys will be boys. Don't defend parents who allow kids to drink in their homes. The law is clear. In my jurisdiction, if you host a party where alcohol is served—even if outside kids bring it—you will be prosecuted. If you allow your own child to drink to the point where he or she harms himself or others, you will be prosecuted.

As if criminal prosecution is not a sufficient deterrent, parents are responsible for civil damages. In other words, if some kid gets loaded at your house, leaves, gets behind the wheel of a car, and ends up in an accident, you're responsible. If there's a wrongful death because of that kid's actions, you're responsible. Even if you're not home, if you have any reason to know that underage drinking is going on in your absence you can be held responsible. Breathtaking, isn't it? Parents are responsible for the behaviors of their children. Whether they want to be or not, whether they are even remotely complicit or not. That's the law.

I have spent the last nine years doing everything within my power, through the law and through education, to stop this plague. Every time I think we've made headway, I am shocked anew by how far we have yet to go.

New Year's Eve 2002. Shortly before midnight, acting on a tip from a concerned parent, police raided a luxury hotel in Westchester. In three connected hotel rooms, they found twenty-six teenagers partying. Their ages ranged from fifteen to nineteen. A large quantity of alcohol and some marijuana was found. Although it was relatively early and the party was just getting started, some of the kids were already heavily intoxicated. One drunken teen was caught stumbling across the rooftop of the six-story hotel. There is little doubt that he was headed for a tragic end if the police had not appeared at that moment and led him away to safety.

All of the teens were taken into custody, and they remained at police headquarters until midmorning New Year's Day while police tried to piece together what had happened.

I was angry and frustrated when I learned about the drinking party. In November we'd held a forum at Manhattanville College on underage drinking. The room had been packed with parents, teenagers, and school administrators. The forum was an intervention in response to an urgent problem in our community, which was reaching crisis proportions. In the months following Robert Viscome's death, there had been several incidents of mass teen drinking that had shocked the community. In September hundreds of students came to a high school homecoming dance in Scarsdale drunk. Many were vomiting in waste cans and passing out.

The New Year's Eve bust was a dispiriting reminder of how deeply entrenched this kind of drinking behavior is among our youth. When I learned how the kids had managed to rent the rooms, I went ballistic.

The host of the party was a nineteen-year-old boy named Kevin McNeill. Kevin's father had helped him secure the hotel rooms after Kevin allegedly promised that there would be no alcohol present. How could a conscientious parent fall for that line? Even if Kevin was sincere, he couldn't be expected to control the actions of twenty-six partygoers. One had to assume that someone would bring booze, especially to a New Year's Eve party. Any parent would suspect that, and Patrick McNeill wasn't just any parent.

Sadly, I remembered the McNeill family very well. In 1997 another son, Patrick, Jr., twenty, had disappeared after a night of heavy drinking at a bar in Manhattan. Friends said the boy was literally falling down drunk when he left the bar. There was a frantic search, but he remained missing. Two months later, his body was found in the waters of New York Harbor. The medical examiner said that, despite all that time in the river, Patrick McNeill's body still contained enough measurable alcohol to fail a drunk driving test.

The grief-stricken McNeill family filed a $20 million lawsuit against the bar, its owners, the bouncer, and the bartender, arguing that all parties knew Patrick was underage, but had served him excessive amounts of alcohol nevertheless. The McNeill family wanted the death of their eldest son to serve as a wake-up call to the community at large.

Given this tragic history, I could hardly believe my ears when I heard that it was Mr. McNeill who had arranged for the hotel rooms. Mr. McNeill defended his decision by saying he trusted his son Kevin and that he'd made sure the minibars in the hotel rooms were locked.

It's time to change our culture. If parents don't realize that underage drinking is a dead end, both literally and figuratively, then perhaps it's time to start making parents criminally responsible for the actions of their underage kids. As the law now stands, without proof that he knew there would be alcohol, Patrick McNeill couldn't be prosecuted.

Was there a public outcry? Did parents, teachers, and community leaders demand action? No, the silence was deafening. One man actually said to me, "Well, you have to have some sympathy for Patrick McNeill. He lost a son."

Whenever I stand in front of a group of parents and speak to them about teenage substance abuse, I am aware of the singular expression that registers on each and every face. It is one of helplessness. I see it in their eyes, in the slump of their shoulders, in the way that they listen but don't really seem to hear. There is always a parent who stands up and asks, "How can we force our kids to do what we tell them?" It makes me wonder why parents today believe they have no influence over their children. Why have the adults ceded control? How can I convince them that the single most important factor in preventing teen drinking and drug use is parental guidance?

A study conducted by SADD (Students Against Destructive Decisions/Students Against Drunk Driving)
shows that many parents either do not believe that their
teen participates in destructive behaviors, or think that
such behaviors are a normal part of growing up. Many
parents also think there is little, if anything, they can do
to influence the choices of their teenagers. More than
half the parents surveyed agreed that drinking is a part of
growing up and that teens will drink no matter what
parents do. Yet, the teenagers surveyed communicated
exactly the opposite. Those who had open and honest
communication with their parents were less likely to engage in risky behaviors. Those whose parents were un-
equivocal in their zero tolerance policies about drinking
and drug use stated that they were less likely to drink or
take drugs.

How about that? Parents do have power. They do
have moral authority. But they have to exercise it.

When our kids are in grammar school and are invited
to a party or a play date, we call the other child's parents
and ask a slew of questions: Who's going to supervise?
Who's picking them up? What will they be doing?
What will they be eating? We even do it for middle
school children. Then, when our kids reach high school,
we back off. They're only fourteen or fifteen years old,
and we act as if they've instantly passed into maturity.
What makes us stop asking about our children's well-
being?

Teenagers have one mission in life: to be independent. As parents we have one obligation: to keep them safe. Those goals are often at cross-purposes, but we must hold firm to our responsibilities. Too many parents today want to be their kids' friends, so they back down. They don't want to disappoint or embarrass them. I tell parents, "Your kids have plenty of friends. They don't need another friend. They need a parent."

At one event a woman in the audience stood up and said, "I used to get involved and call around to find out about parties and events my daughter was going to. But I was the only parent who did it, and my daughter was embarrassed. It wasn't worth the carrying on, so I stopped calling. I was the only one, anyway."

"You're worried about embarrassing your daughter, but that should be the least of your worries," I said. "You should be worried that last year seven million teenagers accepted rides from kids who had been drinking, and your daughter could be one of them. You should be worried that a high percentage of teens have sexual encounters they don't want or plan for when they are drinking. You should be thinking about consequences, not feelings."

According to the National Institute on Alcohol Abuse and Alcoholism, alcohol is used by the perpetrator, the victim, or both in 80 percent of sexual-assault cases. Date rape is a real danger for adolescent girls who drink alcohol or are in situations where alcohol is consumed. In the summer of 2003, we prosecuted a sixteen-year-old boy after he was caught fondling a thirteen-year-old girl who had passed out from alcohol consumption.

The new epidemic in underage drinking has increasingly taken place in affluent communities, where parents are busy with careers. Kids have plenty of disposable income. They can afford to drop seventy-five dollars for fake ID. They have credit cards to put a deposit on a keg. They live in big houses where they can party without anyone watching. They also experience a great deal of competitive pressure, have multiple extracurricular activities, and are in a constant state of panic about getting into a good college. The combination of accessibility and pressure leads to drinking and other dangerous behaviors. The missing link is the parent. A lack of parental control is the major reason for alcohol abuse by underage kids.

Law enforcement may not be able to enforce family values, but we can aggressively investigate and enforce the law to make things very uncomfortable for the people who supply alcohol to kids. This is a policy that every law enforcement agency should adopt. Since 1996, we have been conducting stings in Westchester County. The U.S. Department of Justice cites vigorous use of compliance checks as a very high priority in any effective strategy to reduce underage drinking. Our investigators have joined with several police departments in the county, the state police, and the New York State Liquor Authority. On a recent day, they accompanied teenage undercover operatives, who looked no older than they were, as they attempted to purchase alcohol one hundred and twenty-five times from licensed establishments in Westchester. Two-thirds of the establishments refused to sell them alcohol, but at forty-two locations no one asked for ID before a sale was made. Charges were filed.

Many teens who are asked for proof of age when attempting to purchase alcohol use false IDs. We have launched a crackdown on the use of fake IDs by teenagers. In the course of our post–September 11 investigations into false ID mills, we confiscated from one broker hundreds of so-called "drinker's licenses," created for minors. We also obtained the names of hundreds of teenagers in the county who had purchased IDs from the broker.

We put the word out through the schools and through public service announcements in the media that teenagers with fake IDs would be given a thirty-day amnesty period to surrender them and avoid having their names sent to the commissioner of the Department of Motor Vehicles for possible suspension or revocation of their driver's licenses. It should be a matter of law that anyone using a fraudulent driver's license should have his or her legal license revoked.

I've met with restaurant and tavern owners, and I believe that most establishments don't want to sell alcohol to minors. Time and again we've had people caught in stings at supermarkets, convenience stores, and gas stations who say that they did ask for ID if someone looked underage, but it was hard to tell. The kids looked older. The fake licenses looked real.

I asked my staff to look into acquiring a device that could help proprietors spot phony licenses. The security laminate verifier is a small machine that reveals the laminate security feature on New York drivers' licenses issued after 1997. I wanted to know how much it would cost to get these verifiers for every establishment in the area that sells alcohol. The answer came back: $12,000 for 2,300 verifiers.

I got on the phone to my good friend Ernest McFadden, of Heineken USA. I knew Ernie from his work in the county as a volunteer and town official.

"Only twelve grand to sponsor this program and show that Heineken cares about the kids in our community. It's a real bargain," I told Ernie.

"I like the program, and I'm sure Heineken would be interested," Ernie replied. "I just don't know how fast we can cut through the red tape and get it done."

"I need it now, Ernie. The holidays are coming, and the kids are going to be in a party mode. Maybe I should make another call."

"Who?" he couldn't help asking.

"Budweiser."

"Okay, we'll do it."

With that, Operation Teen Proof was born. Now,

2,300 proprietors in Westchester County have a tool that may help save a kid's life or prevent an injury, a rape, or an assault. Now Heineken is considering expanding the program statewide. It's a small step forward in a long and costly war.

CHAPTER 7

A Serpent's Tooth

The defining image I carry from my childhood is of my mother as a champion of the elderly. It wasn't presented to me as a big deal. In fact, I don't remember my mother ever saying that it was my obligation to help our elderly neighbors who couldn't always do for themselves. It was just an understanding, a given, that once a week we'd take Mrs. LaBert grocery shopping, because she was legally blind and couldn't manage on her own. When we returned to her darkened house, we'd straighten up and stay for a visit. My mother was never in a hurry. She made Mrs. LaBert feel as if there was nothing in the world she'd rather be doing than sitting with her.

It was also a given that once or twice a week I'd spend

a few hours across the street helping Mrs. Fleming, who was very heavy and arthritic. The simplest movements were an ordeal for Mrs. Fleming. She couldn't raise her hand over her head, bend to pick up an item she'd dropped, or open a jar with her stiff, swollen fingers. I'd wash and set her hair and clean her house.

Some of my fondest memories are of sitting with Mrs. Fleming on her broad Victorian porch in the late afternoons, rocking and talking. She was an extremely bright woman, and I learned from her that age and physical disability don't necessarily extinguish the spark of intellect and interest. I realized, even as a young girl, that I probably benefited from knowing Mrs. LaBert and Mrs. Fleming more than they benefited from knowing me.

Because respect for the elderly was so deeply ingrained in me from childhood, it still shocks me when I encounter crimes against the elderly. Any decent human being has to be disgusted by such callousness. It is much harder to face when the abuse occurs in our own homes. Two-thirds of all elder abuse takes place at the hands of family members, usually adult children or an older person's spouse. Domestic violence in a marriage will last into its later years. It doesn't just end as people grow older. If a man abuses his wife when he's forty, he will abuse her when he's seventy. Individuals over the age of eighty suffer the most abuse, especially if they are dependent on others for their daily care.

Abuse takes many forms. Often aging parents are struck, pushed, beaten, drugged, force-fed, or starved by children or grandchildren. Threats, insults, accusations, humiliation, and isolation can be as crippling as physical abuse. Some abused seniors are deprived of eyeglasses, dentures, medical care, and even the means to keep themselves clean.

In many cases, the mistreatment has a financial inducement. I've seen instances of adult children holding their parents hostage, providing them the bare minimum required to keep them alive while plundering their bank accounts, stealing their pension money, and cashing their Social Security checks for their own use. When Shakespeare wrote, "How sharper than a serpent's tooth it is to have a thankless child," he might have been referring to these soulless offspring.

Although much attention has been focused on the maltreatment of seniors in nursing homes, hospitals, and assisted living facilities, the abuse of the elderly at the hands of their own loved ones is a scandal of far greater proportions—and one that has received very little attention.

Shame, fear, and isolation contribute to the secrecy that makes elder abuse one of the most difficult problems to resolve within the criminal justice system. It is extremely rare for an elderly person to report that he or she is being physically or emotionally abused, robbed of their resources, or neglected. Under the shield of family privacy, there are countless unknown victims who spend their final days in terror and misery. Unlike suspected child abuse cases, where hospital personnel are required to report suspicions of abuse, there is no mandate to report suspected instances of elder abuse. Many abused elderly suffer rather than break the family's code of silence. The shame and embarrassment they feel is tremendous.

Imagine having to admit that your son slaps you around, that your daughter withholds food, that your grandchild threatens you. It's hard enough to admit to yourself that such things are possible. Making the abuse public is more than most people can bear. For this reason, many states have attempted to pass legislation mandating that health care providers report suspected abuse to authorities, so there can be intervention by Adult Protective Services. To date, no state has enacted such legislation.

In 1998 the Administration on Aging published its first-ever National Elder Abuse Incident Study. The study estimated that at least a half million older persons suffered abuse in domestic settings in a given year. For every one incident reported, at least five went unreported.

A few private and not-for-profit corporations are breaking new ground in an effort to help law enforcement address elder abuse. For example, in Westchester County, the Hebrew Home for the Aged at Riverdale, under the inspired leadership of Dan Reingold, pioneered a successful training program to educate medical professionals, police, and social workers on the signs of elder abuse and how to intervene on behalf of the victim. However, even when Adult Protective Services, law enforcement, and the courts become involved, there's no guarantee that these tormented men and women will get help. When I was chief of the Domestic Violence/ Child Abuse Unit, I dealt with many elderly people who refused all offers of assistance. I still remember the seventy-two-year-old woman who refused to testify against her son, even though he beat her so badly she was in the hospital for weeks. When I visited her there, she shook her head weakly and said, "Maybe it's my fault. I raised him."

I remember the seventy-year-old diabetic whose thirty-year-old daughter hit him with a hammer because he forgot to take his insulin shot. He, too, declined to press charges. I remember the dignified seventy-eight-year-old woman from a prominent family whose son beat her regularly. This lovely woman went to great lengths to keep that fact from the world. It was too mortifying to discuss publicly. Only when he broke three of her fingers did she reluctantly agree to press charges.

Eighty-year-old Margaret Raffaele did not survive a vicious attack by her forty-eight-year-old son Charles. A violent alcoholic, Charles was often heard by nearby neighbors screaming at his mother in the White Plains apartment they shared. On the night of January 13, 2002, the neighbors heard Margaret screaming and the sounds of a scuffle, but no one called the police until two days later, when Charles was heard making a terrible racket.

When police arrived, they found the battered woman lying on the floor of her bedroom. It was eventually determined that she had been lying there unattended for two days. Hospitalized and treated for her injuries and dehydration, she nevertheless died from a heart attack ten days later.

This case was especially disturbing, because Margaret Raffaele might have been saved if one of her neighbors had picked up the phone and called the police on the fateful night when the assault occurred. It underscores how deadly the combination of violence and isolation can be.

Although his mother did not die until ten days after the original incident, Charles was charged with Second-Degree Murder under the theory that his attack and subsequent disregard for his mother—leaving her on the floor unattended for two days—showed a depraved indifference to human life and created a substantial risk that she would die. In a nonjury trial, the judge acquitted Charles of Murder, finding him guilty of the lesser charge of Manslaughter, which could provide a sentence of as little as five years in prison.

We lack respect for elders in this country. In a disposable society they are the easiest to do away with. We warehouse them in nursing homes, we ignore them, and when they die, their deaths count for little. This is not true in all societies. Native Americans have a cultural imperative to respect the elderly. It is an honor for grown children to care for their parents in old age. In Japan age is synonymous with wisdom. It demands respect. Western society, with its privilege and opportunity, does not have the same mandate.

Elder abuse is on the rise, the predictable outcome of greater longevity. The stresses of caring for elderly parents without adequate financial resources or support services can be too much for families already stretched to the breaking point. We must make a commitment to solve this problem, or we'll face the consequences. When adult children abuse their aging parents, the cycle of violence practically guarantees that they will someday be abused by their own children. And so it goes—until we decide to break the cycle once and for all.

As district attorney, one of the most frustrating crimes I see is elderly people getting scammed for their money. This generation of seniors is extremely careful with every hard-earned cent. They've usually scrimped and saved their entire lives to build their fragile nest eggs. Seniors living on fixed incomes have no safety net. Every day we hear about people making choices between whether to fill a prescription for medicine or to eat dinner. Every penny counts.

Although the elderly are extremely careful with their money, they can still be sitting ducks for financial frauds. According to the Department of Justice, more than one-fourth of all telemarketing frauds are committed against persons over the age of sixty, and the proportion of individuals losing $5,000 or more in Internet schemes is higher for seniors than it is for any other age category. Financial exploitation is the fastest growing form of elderly abuse. Half of all elder abuse cases in New York State involve financial exploitation. These incidents include abuse of power of attorney; misuse of ATMs, credit cards, and bank accounts; appropriation of pensions and benefit checks; illegal property transfers; and con artist scams.

Catherine Martino, thirty-five, conducted a major fraud involving seniors in Westchester, Suffolk, and Brooklyn. Her goal was literally to steal their homes out from under them. Martino operated two companies called BBC Funding Corporation and BBC Properties Portfolio Corporation, with offices on Long Island. Through these companies she posed as a mortgage broker and home-improvement-loan moneylender. Martino targeted senior citizens who owned homes in economically disadvantaged areas and "cold called" them. At the door, she smiled warmly and exerted just enough high-pressure salesmanship to get invited into their homes. There she would turn the pressure up a few notches, convincing them to take out home improvement loans at very low interest rates. When a homeowner agreed, Martino went through a process that appeared to be a standard evaluation, appraisal, and closing. At the "closing" the victim was required to sign a series of papers described as loan documents. Often, the victims were in their eighties and nineties, and they had a hard time reading the fine print. They ended up trusting Martino's assurances. Included among the papers were quitclaim deeds transferring ownership of the house from the victim to Martino or her company. Then Martino filed the quitclaim deed in the county clerk's office and used the new deed to acquire a mortgage or a loan for herself or her company, using the fraudulently acquired deed as collateral. Once she had the money, she defaulted on the mortgage or loan. The victims, who received no money on the phony home improvement loans, only discovered the fraud when the lending institutions started foreclosure proceedings on their homes.

Martino devised a shortcut to the scheme. One elderly Mt. Vernon woman visited by Martino agreed to apply for a $5,000 loan at a low-interest rate. Martino asked to see her property deed and other identifying information. After Martino had left, allegedly to make copies of the documents, the woman noticed paper in her wastebasket on which it appeared that Martino had been practicing her signature! The woman later learned that Martino had forged her signature on the deed, obtained a mortgage on her home, and defaulted in paying the mortgage, placing the woman at risk of foreclosure and eviction.

The investigation into Catherine Martino's scam was conducted by our Economic Crimes Bureau, working closely with the Criminal Investigations Bureau of the

State of New York Banking Department. Martino was arrested, pled guilty to Grand Larceny in the Second Degree, and was sentenced to one to three years in state prison. It seemed a small price to pay for the havoc she created in the lives of her victims.

On December 21, 1999, a Westchester County court ordered that all titles and deeds stolen from the senior citizens through Martino's fraud be returned to the victims. The court further ordered that all mortgages, loans, and other encumbrances obtained by Martino against the stolen properties were void, due to her fraud. This ruling freed the victims and their property from any liability to lending institutions.

We've prosecuted several cases in recent years involving persons who insinuate themselves into the lives of elderly persons living alone, usually posing as caretakers. Kenneth Gragert, thirty-two, was a brazen criminal, highlighting once again how isolation can make the elderly and infirm easy prey for criminals.

Gragert targeted a ninety-seven-year-old man and took over his life, telling others he was the man's caretaker. He moved him out of his house and into Gragert's home. He then proceeded to withdraw large sums of money from the man's brokerage account, certificates of deposit, and savings accounts. He also deposited his victim's retirement checks, which included his Social Security payment, his New York State pension check, and his military pension check into his own bank accounts.

By the time Gragert was apprehended, the old man's finances had been wiped out, and he was at death's door. He died within a year. He didn't live to see Gragert put behind bars for his pitiless criminal manipulation and financial swindle.

Nor did O. Winston Link live to see the ultimate fate of his life's work. Link, one of America's foremost photographers of steam locomotives, was in his late seventies when his wife Conchita held him a virtual prisoner while she carted away more than $2 million worth of his classic photographs. We prosecuted and convicted her of Grand Larceny, and she was sentenced to and served a lengthy prison term. Link's photographs were never recovered, and Conchita adamantly refused to give up the goods. In 2001, Link died at the age of eighty-six, the whereabouts of his life's work and historical contribution still unknown.

Then, in 2003, we received a call that some of Link's photographs had surfaced on eBay. They were being sold by a New York antiques dealer. When we contacted the dealer, he told us he'd been approached by Conchita and her new husband about selling the photographs. He'd never questioned the legitimacy of their ownership, but now he was willing to cooperate fully with our investigation. With his help, we arranged a sting. He told Conchita that a corporation was interested in purchasing thirty photographs to use in the redecoration of their corporate headquarters. Conchita bit, and we recovered thirty classic works. A search warrant for Conchita's Gettysburg, Pennsylvania, home yielded no additional pictures, but my investigators did find a rental receipt for a self-storage facility.

There we found a motherload of O. Winston Link's work. A priceless piece of Americana was restored to Link's heirs and to the nation.

There is a special place in hell reserved for criminals who commit violence against the elderly. They are the worst kind of cowards, choosing their victims because they're frail and vulnerable and can't fight back.

Few crimes shock the public conscience like the rape of an elderly woman. It's a jarring event that challenges every stereotype people have about the nature of rape, reminding them that rape is not just a sex crime; it is a crime of violence—a means of exerting power and control. As you can well imagine, rape takes an especially heavy emotional toll on elderly women—one from which they may never recover.

These women were raised in an era when sexual matters were not discussed. Their perspectives were molded from a rigid morality. They were likely to be somewhat judgmental toward rape victims—believing that they had played a role in provoking the attack. When they are raped, the violation rips apart their framework for living, their dignity, and their self-image.

I remember one seventy-four-year-old woman who was raped by the handyman in her apartment building. She was so ashamed, she didn't report it. She actually believed it was her fault because she had been friendly to the man. She nursed her physical and emotional wounds in silence for two days after the attack. On the third day, her daughter came to visit and was alarmed when she saw the bruises on her mother's face, and the way she moved gingerly, as if in pain. At first her mother refused to tell her what had happened, but finally she broke down, and between sobs, choked out the details of the attack.

"My heart was broken," the daughter told me. "She kept saying she shouldn't have talked to him, shouldn't have been so friendly. She thought she had led him on! My mother didn't know how else to process this event. She thought rape only happened to girls in miniskirts, who brought it on themselves."

We arrested and prosecuted this woman's attacker, but we could not restore her sunny disposition, sense of trust, or natural sociability. After the incident she rarely left her apartment. She was forever changed, emotionally scarred by the rape.

Imagine being awakened in the night by the sound of shattering glass as a burglar breaks into your home. This happened to one ninety-six-year-old man who lived alone. He called out from his bed in confusion and fear, and the burglar, thirty-two-year-old Kristopher Gaffney, entered the bedroom and hit the trembling man repeatedly. He then wrapped a telephone wire around the frail man's throat and choked him until he lost consciousness. It wasn't the first burglary Gaffney had committed in the dead of night. At least one other victim, a ninety-two-year-old woman, suffered the same fate. What a coward Gaffney was to select as his victims men and women in their nineties!

Imagine, too, stopping to ask for directions on the street, and being beaten senseless. That's what happened to Alberto Reyes, a seventy-six-year-old gentleman who was strolling along Warburton Avenue in Yonkers, New York, on October 29, 1994. Reyes approached a group of four young people, a man and three women, and politely asked one of the women for directions. Before she could reply, the man in the group, twenty-six-year-old Linwood Lockley, punched Reyes in the face. The elderly man fell to the ground. Lockley began kicking him repeatedly in the head and face. He then started stomping on Reyes's head with both feet, as the three women screamed for him to stop. How many blows in all? According to one of the women, there were "too many to count."

Finally, the attack ended. Lockley was walking away when he noticed he had a cut on his hand. Furious, he turned and delivered several more kicks to Reyes's face and head. Later, when he was arrested, Lockley told police, "I didn't do anything. All I did was smack the guy."

Alberto Reyes was so battered by Lockley's brutal assault that doctors had to remove his left eye to prevent

an infection to the brain. Nonetheless, Reyes never recovered. Within a month, he contracted pneumonia and
died. We prosecuted Linwood Lockley for murder. He
was convicted and sentenced to a term of twenty-five
years to life.

Every citizen has a right to feel safe in his or her own
neighborhood, and senior citizens have a right to enjoy
their golden years without terror. We have yet to reach a
point where that right can be guaranteed. Indeed, every
person convicted of a crime against a person over age
sixty-five should face an additional period of imprisonment because of the vulnerability of the victim. It would
amount to a statement of policy that we revere our seniors and will protect them with stiff sanctions against
their attackers. It would be society's way of stating un-
equivocally that we will not tolerate the victimization of
these men and women, who should be held in the highest esteem. I grieve for our inability to protect elderly
men like Charles Guardino, who was murdered in his
own home.

October 13, 1999, was Charles Guardino's ninety-
first birthday. He was as fit as a man his age could be. At
three that afternoon, he was enjoying a mild fall day by
raking leaves in his front yard. Around him buzzed the
familiar activities of midafternoon in Shenorock, New
York—a school bus dropping off children, the sounds of
laughter and play.

Suddenly, Guardino's afternoon peace was shattered
by the appearance of a neighbor, nineteen-year-old Kon-

stantin Kojinsky, who was holding a 9mm rifle. Kojinsky was agitated, and he had been drinking heavily. He grabbed Guardino's rake and threw it to the ground. He demanded Guardino's car keys, then shoved the old man across the yard and into his house, in the process knocking out his hearing aid. There he threatened Guardino's daughter-in-law and stole Guardino's wallet.

Guardino's dog, disturbed by the scene, began barking. As Guardino watched helplessly, Kojinsky shot and wounded his dog. Then he turned the rifle on the old man. "Don't shoot!" Guardino cried, seconds before Kojinsky shot him three times, killing him.

The crime was so senseless, so appalling, that the community was in an uproar. There was momentum building for our office to seek the death penalty against Kojinsky. I gave the matter serious consideration and looked into all of the aggravating and mitigating circumstances. In the end, Kojinsky's age and mental problems mitigated against the death penalty. He pled guilty to murder in the first degree and received a sentence of twenty-five years to life. Was it enough? It's never enough. There's no fair exchange for a man's life.

In 1995 a number of seniors living alone in single-family homes in Westchester County were the victims of push-in robberies and assaults. One elderly man in Greenburgh died from his injuries. None of the victims could identify the attacker. We launched a coordinated hunt for the perpetrator, which involved the forty-four police departments in the county, as well as the police from other New York and New Jersey neighborhoods experiencing similar crimes.

Fortunately, one brave woman lived to help us put this creep away. Margaret Brigham is my hero. She's an example of the indomitable spirit of her generation, and the power of focused, activist outrage.

Margaret was eighty-six the day a strange man rang her doorbell in the scenic village of Ossining and said he was looking for work. He told her he'd done work at her house many years ago with his father. Margaret knew he'd never been there before, and she declined. Then he asked for a glass of water. Realizing Margaret was alone, he entered the home and pushed Margaret down a long flight of stairs to the basement. He ran down after her, yanked her wedding and engagement rings off of her hand, and then dragged her to a closet under the basement stairs, where he locked her in. Margaret was covered with bruises. Her left arm had been broken, and she was in a great deal of pain. Remarkably, she was not severely injured. She sat in the closet and listened to the intruder ransacking her house and yelling out to her, "Where's your money? Where's your money?" Finally he fled her home, leaving her for dead.

Margaret knew she might indeed die if she didn't find a way out of the closet. She grabbed a metal vacuum cleaner rod and began to pound on the door. Her pounding miraculously jarred the door open. She hobbled up the basement stairs, got to her phone, and called 911.

Margaret would prove invaluable in helping us nail the man who had been preying on seniors throughout the area. She was sharp as a tack, and gave the police sketch artist a dead-on description of her assailant. Police eventually picked up Larry Stevens of Staten Island, and Margaret was able to single him out in a police lineup.

She was one spunky woman. She came to the office and we all fell in love with her. She was everybody's grandmother—a soft cloud of white hair, a lovely manner, and kind blue eyes. We talked about her case, and Margaret didn't have the slightest hesitation about testifying. She knew it was up to her as the only victim who could clearly identify Stevens. "I'll tell them what he did to me," she said firmly. "He won't do this again."

I went to court on the day she testified. She looked frail and tiny on the stand. I smiled to myself, knowing how deceiving looks can be. When the defense attorney questioned her, she was very condescending. She spoke loudly, in a slow drawl, as if she were addressing an impaired child. "Mrs. Brigham, did you have your glasses on? . . . Mrs. Brigham, do you have memory problems? . . . Mrs. Brigham, do you ever get confused?" She was drawing it out, trying to shake Margaret up and make her look uncertain.

Margaret stared back at her, cool and unflappable. She answered in a clear, strong voice. "I know it was him. I'll never forget those beady eyes." And I thought, *Way to go, Margaret!*

She came to the office to thank me after Larry Stevens was convicted. By that time she was like part of the family. I asked her, "Margaret, I'm curious. Why did you open the door for this guy? You see what an animal he is."

She said, "If I had seen those beady eyes, I would never have opened the door."

Her response sparked an idea. If there was one thing I knew about seniors, it was that they could read people. What if we gave them a chance to do that before they opened their doors? Margaret's comment was the genesis of my Watchful Eye program.

I gathered my assistant DAs and told them, "As a community service project we are going to install peepholes in the doors of senior citizens." I got on the phone and started calling corporations for donations, and my good friend, David Pecker, who at that time was with Hachette Filipacchi Media, U.S., immediately donated enough money to fund the purchase of five hundred peepholes. We brought in a master craftsman to teach us how to drill a wood door, a metal door, a hollow door, and install the peepholes.

It has been a highly successful program. When we go out to put in a peephole, it gives us the opportunity to talk to the seniors, tell them about our office, and make suggestions about ways they can protect themselves. So far, my assistant DAs have installed more than one thousand peepholes. We have no idea how many crimes may have been prevented because of Margaret's courage and fortitude, but thanks to her, many other seniors are safer today. I think every peephole we install should come with a sticker: "Courtesy of Margaret Brigham."

My mother, Esther Ferris, is seventy-two now. She lives alone in the small town where I grew up, where she tends her garden, grows her own vegetables, and continues to quietly spread her charity to those in need. She is a model of what it means to age with dignity, strength, and beauty. This tiny woman, with a stature that transcends her physical size, greets every day with a glowing smile that welcomes the world. Her character and grace that made such an impression on me when I was young now provides a vision for me of what it means to grow older.

There is nothing frail about my mother. She is alert, savvy, and she stands her ground. She knows that there are people who try to take advantage of older women, but I pity the predator who tries to put anything over on Esther Ferris. She takes no bunk from anybody. I aspire to be like her. I aspire, too, to live in a society that comes to value the living treasure of our elder population.

CHAPTER 8

Mean Streak

On the afternoon of September 11, 2001, with the smoky haze from the collapsed World Trade Center towers drifting north along the Hudson River, thirty-four-year-old Steven Montemurro walked into a little delicatessen in Ardsley, New York, and confronted the owner. "Are you an Arab?" he demanded to know, obviously angry. When the man replied that he was, Montemurro let loose with a volley of racist epithets. As the deli's other workers, also Arabs, cowered behind the counter, the owner firmly ordered Montemurro to leave. Enraged anew, still screaming slurs, Montemurro produced a can of pepper spray and sprayed the deli owner in the face. The victim required a trip to the hospital to treat his burning eyes and skin. The injury to his psyche, his sense of safety and well-being, would take far longer to heal.

Montemurro made a clear choice. Because of the horrific events that occurred on September 11, 2001, he decided that it was okay for him to walk into that deli and hold its owner personally responsible for the actions of a group of terrorists. The terrorists were Arabs, and the deli owner was an Arab. That was good enough for Montemurro. It was an act of pure hate.

Hate crimes foment in the stunted minds of the ignorant and the arrogant. How ironic that these crimes are often committed in the name of patriotism. They are inherently inhuman and anti-American, the antithesis of patriotism.

We prosecuted Montemurro. Sadly, he wasn't alone. In the six-month period following September 11, the American-Arab Anti-Discrimination Committee received reports of six hundred violent incidents directed against Arab-Americans in the United States. These included acts of physical violence, vandalism, arson, beatings, assault with weapons, and direct threats of specific acts of violence. Human Rights Watch reported a 1,700 percent increase in reported hate and bias crimes against Arabs, Muslims, and those perceived to be Arabs, in the year after the terrorist attack. At least three individuals, and possibly as many as seven, were murdered as the result of the anti-Arab backlash.

Every true American is appalled and ashamed. These hateful acts are not about exacting any form of just ven-

geance. They are about victimizing innocent people—
complete strangers who trigger violent responses because of others' deep-seated fears and biases.

We must begin to deal with this sad truth: There are
people and groups of people interwoven throughout
our diverse communities who rise every day with a terrible hatred burning in their hearts. In 2001 there were
nearly ten thousand hate and bias crimes reported to the
FBI, and this number is believed to be only a fraction of
the crimes committed. By their very nature hate crimes
involve intimidation, and most victims are afraid to
come forward for fear of further consequences. Once
the victims of attack, parents fear for their children; husbands fear for their wives. Entire communities live in
frightened anticipation of further attack.

Is it any wonder that the victims of bias crimes hesitate
to seek assistance from the police or other law enforcement agencies? Their survival instincts, born of experience, tell them that the police can only do so much. No
one expects the police to park a squad car in front of
their homes and watch over a family day and night.

Who commits hate crimes? The perpetrators are overwhelmingly white males. By all accounts, they usually appear to be solid upstanding citizens, loyal and patriotic
Americans. They live in leafy suburban neighborhoods,
have wives and children, hold responsible jobs. They are
active in the PTA, the Neighborhood Watch, and the
volunteer fire department. They are your neighbors and

your neighbor's children. Beneath their upright exteriors, those who commit hate crimes are engaging in their own form of terrorism, and they deserve the same treatment we reserve for enemies of the state.

Hate is the daily fare of a district attorney. I have prosecuted a man who stabbed another man simply because he was of Hispanic origin; another who stabbed his victim, specifically because he was Dominican. I have prosecuted a man who slashed a person's face because he hated minorities. I prosecuted boys who desecrated a synagogue with Nazi symbols and graffiti. I have prosecuted cases against a man who beat three people with a baseball bat, a second who attacked a young man with a box cutter, and a third who shot a man in the hand—in all of those cases, solely because the victims were African-American.

A hate crime is a dagger held to all our throats. It is personal and it includes any member of the targeted group—any African-American, Jew, Arab, homosexual, and so on. Hate crimes are sociopathic acts and warrant very specific kinds of punishment. I have long been an advocate of legislation that would create more stringent penalties for crimes that are committed solely motivated by a person's race, color, national origin, ancestry, gender, religion, age, disability, or sexual orientation.

In 1999 New York was one of the few states that had

not passed some form of hate crime legislation. The senate and assembly would not agree on a uniform approach. It was outrageous that, in New York State— home of Ellis Island and The Statue of Liberty—we didn't have legislation covering hate crimes. For eleven straight years the New York assembly had passed legislation, and for eleven straight years the senate had buried it because the phrase "sexual orientation" was included in the language. Narrow-minded agendas kept the legislation from becoming reality. In 1999 I was elected to a one-year term as president of the New York State District Attorneys Association. One of my top priorities was to pressure the legislature to stop stonewalling on the hate crimes legislation. We needed it to do our jobs more effectively and to protect the victims of such crimes.

Many were either unsure about hate crimes legislation or adamantly opposed to it. Why did we need a specific statute focusing on hate crimes? Is it right, because of the underlying motivation, to treat a crime against one individual more severely than we would treat a similar crime against someone else? Should there be a specific category for "special" victims of crime?

A hate crime is not a crime against a "special" victim. It's a crime against a community of victims. Those who victimize an entire community deserve more punishment than those whose crime is directed against a single individual.

If a man gets into a personal dispute with his neighbor

and takes out a gun and shoots him it's certainly a crime. Hatred, or at least hate-filled rage, is involved. But it does not necessarily create an atmosphere of fear and danger for all other men. A hate crime is grievous not only because it does harm to an individual, but because its effect is to do harm to an entire group of people. Every member of that group fears that they are within the hate criminal's zone of danger.

One night in 1998, two white men in Albany, New York, went driving around in a community whose population was primarily African-American for the sole purpose of finding a person to shoot. They spotted a woman walking down the street—who happened to be a nurse returning home from work—and shot her in the neck. That was a pure hate crime, and it instilled fear in the entire community.

Hate crimes are also different because of the kind of people committing them. What does it say about the character of a person who would assault or threaten someone just because they were black or Jewish or gay? Isn't he more likely to repeat his crime when encountering another member of the group he so hates? Hate is a disease. We need to stop the carriers before they spread their sickness.

As a nation that celebrates and is defined by our diversity, it is vital that we demonstrate a strong and uncompromising public policy that underscores our absolute commitment to freedom. Our country is known around the world as the cradle of liberty, the oldest working democracy in existence. We cannot tolerate people being targeted because they are different. We will not dehumanize people by judging their worth based on the color of their skin or ethnic heritage, their religion, age, sexuality, or their mental or physical disability. Hate crimes strike at our very core, the elemental reason people came from all over the world to become Americans in the first place.

In 1999, as I was lobbying the New York State legislature for the passage of hate crimes legislation, Congress was considering federal legislation. I was invited by senators Orrin Hatch and Ted Kennedy to testify at a hearing before the Senate Judiciary Committee. They wanted the perspective of a local prosecutor.

As I sat before the committee, I testified that I was normally concerned about the proliferation of companion federal crime statutes in those areas where local statutes were sufficient. The vast majority of crimes are prosecuted locally, and that's the way it should be. Local and state officials are directly accountable to the community; but when it came to hate crimes, I believed a federal law was appropriate. In our nation's history there have been other moments when individual states were unwilling to address vital matters of civil rights. At those times, the federal government stepped in to insure equal protection to all of its citizens. This was one of those times.

Also testifying before the Senate Judiciary Committee

that day was Judy Shepard, the mother of Matthew Shepard, a young man who had been murdered in Wyoming the previous year because he was gay. Matthew Shepard was lured out of a bar by two men who pretended to be gay. They beat, robbed, and pistol-whipped the young man, then left him tied to a fence out in the freezing cold. He wasn't found for another eighteen hours. He died five days later. Since Matthew's death, Judy Shepard had become a crusader against hate crimes. At the hearing, when one senator expressed his fear that hate crimes legislation would lead to violations of people's First Amendment rights, Judy spoke up, stating, "I can assure opponents of this legislation, firsthand, it was not words or thoughts but violent actions that killed my son."

In late 1999, Congress passed the Hate Crimes Prevention Act. It was a start, but only that. The federal law did not protect victims of hate crimes based on gender, sexual orientation, or disability. In addition, federal jurisdiction would only be triggered under two circumstances: When a crime occurred while the victim was enjoying a federally protected right, like voting or serving on a jury; or when a crime interfered with the victim's ability to engage in a similar right. It was a rather narrow approach. Efforts in Congress to make the law more inclusive have thus far failed.

In 2000, New York State finally passed hate crime legislation, increasing the penalties for crimes motivated by bias. The bill included crimes targeting gays and lesbians.

To date, a total of forty-three states plus the District of Columbia have provisions in their criminal codes that deal with some form of bias-motivated or hate crime. Only twenty-two states and the District of Columbia punish hate crimes motivated by sexual orientation, and four states plus the District of Columbia include punishment for crimes based on gender identity. All state laws involve a heightened penalty for bias crimes, but the scope of hate crimes laws vary from state to state. Some states follow the federal model and require that the bias act be related to some interference with a state or federally granted right.

For example, in Tennessee, a person who assaults a Hispanic person to prevent that person from voting could be subject to prosecution under the state's hate crimes statute. However, a person who assaults a Hispanic person solely on the basis of ethnicity would not be charged under the hate crime statute. Almost all penalty provisions have the same effect: to punish to a greater degree crime that is motivated by bias. The differences are in how the specific statutes arrive at that effect. The wide variations in state statutes, along with the absence of any statutes in seven states, demonstrates how ambivalent we remain as a nation to the consequences of hate.

According to the Intelligence Project of the Southern Poverty Law Center, which has tracked bias crimes since the 1960s, there are 676 organized hate groups known to be operating in the United States today. Of these groups, 109 are offshoots of the Ku Klux Klan, 209 are neo-Nazis, 43 are racist skinheads, 31 are Christian Identity (a racist religion), 124 are neo-Confederate, 51 are black separatist, and 109 subscribe to a mélange of hate-based ideologies.

It should be no surprise that these groups have found a fertile source for expansion on the Internet, where they launch constant appeals to the children of our nation. Just as with pedophiles, hate groups using the Internet can now directly reach out to any child with a home computer. These hate sites are often flagrantly deceptive. Many attempt to disguise their true message under a thin veneer of religiosity, patriotism, and respectability. They employ manipulation, slander, and lies to make their twisted ideas sound almost reasonable. They are also quick to prey on the rebellious spirit and sense of alienation that delineate many of the teenage years.

A horribly alarming aspect of Internet hate-mongering specifically targeted at teenagers is the growing influence of the white power music industry. The record label Resistance Records has more than three hundred CDs that can be purchased online, with titles like *Coon* and *White Patriot*. In 2002, Resistance Records released a video game called *Ethnic Cleansing,* where players are encouraged to gun down blacks, Hispanics, and Jews.

I began to investigate hate groups and their influence on our kids several years ago, working with the Simon Wiesenthal Center. Through the Center I met a man named T. J. Leyden, a former racist skinhead who saw the light and completely reformed. Leyden's change of heart can only be described as a road-to-Damascus moment.

By the age of thirty he had spent fifteen years in the skinhead movement, was married to a fellow racist, and was on the way to raising his two children to believe in his code of hate. One morning he was watching cartoons with his children, when his three-year-old son got up and turned off the television. "Mom says we can't watch shows with niggers on them," the boy explained. Leyden recalls that hearing his son talk that way "hit me like a ton of bricks. I knew I was taking him down a path where he'd end up in jail or dead, remembered for something horrible like the Oklahoma bombing. All of a sudden I didn't want him to be like me." In that moment, Leyden's life changed.

Leyden has made it his mission in life to fight against hate. He is the only known former skinhead to leave the movement and keep his own name. In addition to his work with the Simon Wiesenthal Center, Leyden has held training sessions on hate groups for law enforcement agencies across the country. He has traveled across the nation, speaking to more than 650,000 students. In his campus program, "Turning Away from Hate," Leyden recounts his remarkable story and helps students understand the harmful culture of hate from which he escaped.

In consultation with Leyden, I learned about the insidious methods hate groups use to draw in young people. Following his parents' divorce, Leyden became a skinhead at the age of fifteen. He was miserable, lonely, and needed to lash out. For the skinhead recruiters he was the perfect candidate—an isolated, angry young white man who desperately needed some sort of community. They made him a member of their tribe. Leyden dropped out of school and began hanging out with skinheads.

Leyden told me that alcohol was a central element at all of the meetings. The kids would get drunk. Then, fueled by alcohol and hate talk, they would go out and prowl their neighborhoods looking for blacks, Hispanics, or "long-hairs," and stomp them bloody with their steel-toed boots. They defined their patriotism by these acts. In adulthood, Leyden grew to be the leader of the pack. His main task was recruiting kids. He and his companions focused on junior high school students because they were the most vulnerable age group.

When Leyden was active in the hate movement, the Internet did not exist. Recruiting was handled one-on-one. The advent of the Internet was a bonanza. It gave the hate groups access to millions of potential new converts.

The World Church of the Creator, a racist, anti-Semitic organization with dozens of Web sites, hosts specially designed programs meant to appeal to kids and teens. The *WCOTC Kids!* site, which is subtitled, "Creativity for Children," features coloring pages and crossword puzzles designed to teach lessons about the fight of the white race against all others. At its *Teens* site, there is an interactive message board and articles written by racist white teens. The site also includes violent images of brutally murdered African-Americans and Jews.

At WCOTC's *Skinheads of Racial Holy War* site, visitors must click "OK" in a window that states "Whites Only" before entering the site where they are greeted by a giant skinhead crushing a tiny Hasidic Jew in his closed fist.

The leader, or "Pontifex Maximus," of the World Church of the Creator, is Matt Hale, thirty-one. I've had the distasteful opportunity to discuss the issue of hate with Mr. Hale on a television program hosted by Johnny Cochran. Fortunately, we were in separate studios. Hale is a clean-cut, articulate young man who carefully chooses his words, attempting to make the violent ideas he spews sound almost reasonable. His eyes are shiny with a zealot's fervor. Scary. "We're not preaching hate," he protests. "We're teaching pride." He and others of his ilk are the most dangerous variety of hatemonger. They seem polite, so our response is also polite. If listened to carefully enough, the message is a sick diatribe on the supremacy of the white race.

In January 2003, Matt Hale was arrested for allegedly trying to have Chicago-based U.S. District Judge Joan Lefkow murdered. The judge had presided over a trademark case Matt Hale's group had lost. For Hale's organization and others like them, he is a martyr to the cause of the racial holy war. Unfortunately, Hale's arrest and the surrounding publicity probably increased the membership of the World Church of the Creator.

Publicity, even when it seems off-putting to the average person, is an effective recruitment tool for hate groups. Leyden recalled an incident that occurred in 1988 when he was still in the movement. At the time, Tom Metzger, founder of the White Aryan Resistance, and his son Jon, were key players. Jon Metzger appeared on the Geraldo Rivera show to debate Roy Innis of the Congress of Racial Equality. A fistfight broke out and Rivera suffered a broken nose. The telephone lines of the White Aryan Resistance lit up with new members. "After that," said Leyden, "when somebody said he joined in 1988, we knew he was a Geraldo skin."

The story gave me a chill. Although substantial research exists that links exposure to violence on television with increased aggression by young people, we allow and even support the high ratings of trash TV. The American Psychological Association has reported that an average child will have witnessed 8,000 murders and 100,000 other acts of violence on television before the end of elementary school. More than one million kids watch *The Jerry Springer Show* every day to revel in the foul language, crass sexual references, and staged violence. Do we think it's okay for our kids to view programs with themes like "Angry Goth Rockers with Weapons," or "Buck-Wild Women"?

Our children are also listening to increasingly violent music that perpetuates negative stereotypes about women and minorities. Research has shown that adolescents who are exposed to violent music videos later express a greater acceptance of violence, and there is a higher probability that they will take part in violence. Those who are exposed to violent music videos are also more accepting of violence toward women.

Many video games also glorify violence, and although they are rated for mature audiences, we know that kids can easily procure the worst of the lot, for example "Grand Theft Auto: Vice City," a PlayStation 2 game that allows players to hijack police cars, gun down pedestrians, kill policemen, and pick up prostitutes in order to get "health points."

These ugly forms of entertainment saturate our culture, and anyone who doesn't think they have an influence is blind. I shudder to think of the kind of society we might become with a population raised on this garbage. Yet, we do little to stop it. Why? The First Amendment protects it as speech. Once again we wrap obscene violence in the flag of this great nation and deliver it to our children as entertainment. Shame on us.

A mean streak runs through the main body of our society like an artery, pumping venom rather than blood. That mean streak is rarely overt, but very much alive.

When a truly shocking act occurs, we react with horror. We're much more comfortable treating it as an isolated incident, the work of a truly evil individual. If we admit that it is more than that, we have to accept our own complicity in allowing hate and violence to flourish in our homes and communities.

The 1996 murder of Charles Campbell represents for me the dangers of buried hatreds that exist beneath a thin veneer of civility. Campbell's murder was viewed by many, including the police, as a hate crime—the shooting death of a black man by a white off-duty police officer. I'm not certain it fit the technical definition of a hate crime. It did, however, fit the societal profile of racial hatred that is still all too common in America. Violence is often triggered by an incident involving an African-American man behaving with a sense of casual entitlement. Such behavior is offensive to white racists. It unhinges them. In the blink of an eye, the violence has escalated. Sometimes it ends in death. That's what happened to thirty-seven-year-old Charles Campbell.

Charles Campbell grew up in Elmsford, New York, where he played football in high school. He wasn't that big or fast, but he played hard. Everyone who knew Charles agreed that he had a good attitude and was well liked. He attended Morgan State University in Maryland, fell in love, and had a child. He left school after two years and returned home when both his parents became ill. Campbell got a job with the White Plains

Sanitation Department, joined a gym in Yonkers, and worked part-time as a recreation counselor at the St. Christopher's–Jennie Clarkson Child Care Home for troubled teenagers.

He had a great reputation there, always putting in extra hours off the books. The kids loved and respected him. They liked his soft-spoken manner. So did Vanessa Maldonado, Campbell's fiancée. The couple had just purchased a home in Hartsdale, and they were planning their wedding.

On October 3, 1996, Campbell put in his regular shift with the Sanitation Department, came home, and took a nap. It was a Thursday, and Campbell usually worked a shift at the home for troubled teens. Not that day. Hours had been cut. He figured he'd go in anyway, have a quick meeting with his boss, and pick up his paycheck. He also wanted to get in a workout at his gym in Yonkers, so he sped off in his shiny new black Corvette, which he'd only recently bought after years of driving one clunker after another.

A counselor who saw him around 4:30 P.M. later described him as being happy and full of laughs. He talked to some other people, then left for the gym in Yonkers. On his way there he decided to stop at Laura's Pizza Den on Ashford Avenue in Dobbs Ferry and grab a slice. He pulled into the only spot he could find, a small private parking lot that serves a mini-mall across from Laura's. He got out in front of the Venice Deli and started across the street.

He was stopped by the owner of the deli, fifty-three-year-old Richard B. DiGuglielmo, who told him to move his car. DiGuglielmo hated it when people who weren't his customers parked in front of his store. It was a small area, and parking was tight. Campbell tried to placate the deli owner. He told him that as soon as he got his slice from Laura's, he'd come into the Venice Deli and buy his soft drink there.

DiGuglielmo still wasn't agreeable, and he threatened to put a big sticker on Campbell's car window.

Undeterred, Campbell went across the street to Laura's Pizza Den and ordered his slice. Before it could be served, the counterman alerted him that DiGuglielmo was putting a sticker on his car. Campbell ran out of the pizzeria and raced across the street to confront the deli owner.

At that point, the deli owner's son, Richard D. DiGuglielmo, thirty-one, an off-duty New York City police officer, came rushing out of the deli, and a fight ensued. He was soon joined by his brother-in-law, thirty-eight-year-old equipment operator Robert W. Errico. During the fight, Campbell was wrestled to the ground, held down, and punched repeatedly, then struck with his own cell phone.

There was a brief pause. Campbell managed to regain his feet, pull himself away, open his car's trunk, and grab an aluminum baseball bat. However, DiGuglielmo Sr. kept yelling at Campbell, who, while backing away, swung the bat low and struck Richard B. DiGuglielmo on the leg. In the meantime, DiGuglielmo's son had rushed into the deli, found the Colt .32-caliber semiautomatic gun kept beneath the register, and ran back outside. He did not warn, he did not command Charles Campbell to put down the aluminum bat. He raised the pistol and, from a distance of almost twenty feet, fired three shots into Charles Campbell's torso. All three rounds were fatal.

Paramedics were called at around 5:15 P.M. and Campbell was rushed to Dobbs Ferry Hospital, less than a mile from the Venice Deli. He was officially pronounced dead at the hospital at 5:34 P.M. Richard D. DiGuglielmo was arrested. Afterward DiGuglielmo repeatedly claimed that he shot Campbell "to save my father's life."

I didn't buy it. Many witnesses said that Campbell was behaving in a defensive manner, backing off as he held the bat, moving well out of anyone's range when the shots were fired. The self-defense claim simply did not ring true. In addition to the bullet wounds that killed him, Campbell's body bore the marks of a beating. Richard D. DiGuglielmo and Robert Errico were stocky men with thick, tattooed biceps. The father Richard D. would claim to be "saving" was not a doddering old man. He was fifty-three years old and in good physical shape.

The bereaved family and friends of Charles Campbell filled my office, trying to make sense of what was ultimately senseless. They wanted to know why this unthinkable tragedy happened. Richard D. DiGuglielmo was a police officer. How could he have fired those shots? Why didn't he shout a warning? Chaz wasn't violent. He wasn't crazy. He was just trying to get away. I had no answers for their questions.

Chaz's twelve-year-old son, Vaughn, tearfully mourned the years he would live without his dad, and the sports he would play that his dad would never watch. Vanessa cried for the shattered dream of a wedding, a home, and a life with the man she loved. I thought about the ripple effect of this man's death, affecting all of the lives Charles Campbell had touched.

Charles's brother and fiancée came regularly to the trial, and many concerned citizens from the African-American community accompanied them. I often heard people express doubt that a white police officer could be convicted for the murder of an African-American. They felt disenfranchised from the criminal justice system, left out of the social contract, and embittered by their collective disappointments. On Memorial Day, I marched in the Yonkers parade, and people held up signs and called out, "Justice for Charles Campbell!"

In my mind, the facts surrounding Campbell's death spoke for themselves. They spoke of the combustible confluence of hatred and ignorance that propels some people to acts of violence, even murder. They spoke of a long history of racial disparity in the delivery of justice for an entire class of citizens—and of a country still afflicted with the vestiges of slavery, lynching, and systemic racial discrimination.

Richard D. DiGuglielmo, the police officer, the

shooter, was convicted of Murder with Depraved Indifference. DiGuglielmo could have received twenty-five years to life, but the judge in the case reduced it to twenty, stating that the shooting "was the product of his genuine love and concern for his father."

Even with the conviction, some members of the African-American community refused to believe it was real or that it would stick. I remember a woman who came up to me after DiGuglielmo was sentenced, and she said with absolute conviction, "The verdict will be reversed on appeal."

"Let's make a wager," I said. "Give me your name and address. If this verdict is reversed, I'll send you ten dollars." She laughed, and I'm sure she thought I was kidding. But when the verdict was upheld by the appellate court, I wrote to her to let her know that justice had, indeed, been done.

Had Campbell not been an African-American driving a Corvette, would there have been an objection to his parking in front of the deli, promising to buy a soda there after he got his pizza? Had Campbell been white, would any shots have been fired? The bullets that slammed into Charles Campbell's torso and ended his life were not fired out of love. They were fired in hate.

Hate is an infectious disease. Over time, it can spread until it becomes the dominant culture of a society. We like to think that's impossible in America, but we cannot

afford to grow complacent. Other societies, once as civilized as we are, have been overrun and nearly destroyed
by the insidious tide of hate. We are not immune.

In 1999 my office was asked by the U.S. Department
of State to participate in a volunteer program to interview Kosovar refugees being housed at Fort Dix in New
Jersey. The interviews were part of a United Nations effort to gather evidence of genocide in the prosecution
of Serbian war criminals.

Accompanied by three fine prosecutors from my office—Barbara Egenhauser, veteran sex crimes prosecutor; Steven Vandervelden, organized crime bureau chief;
and Michael Hughes, my public integrity bureau chief
(Mike was a captain in the Judge Advocate General's
Corps of the U.S. Navy Reserves)—I spent a week at
Fort Dix, talking to more than one hundred refugees
through an interpreter. The language barrier did not
prevent us from seeing the horrors they had suffered in
the name of ethnic cleansing.

It was immediately clear that this wasn't about war. It
was about a massive hate crime perpetrated against Muslims. The victims told us about the way soldiers, para-
military, and even marauding civilians, would burst into
people's homes, massacre entire families, and burn their
houses to the ground. I interviewed a man who saw his
brother beaten to death with a wooden glove with iron
knuckles and the butt of a gun. He saw two other brothers have their fingernails pulled off, then their fingers
cut off, before being killed.

The refugees talked about masses of people being ordered to leave the country, of being crammed into boxcars and sent to Macedonia, of babies born on train platforms being trampled. They told us how the men in their households were dragged out and thrown into trenches, while the women stayed inside and listened to their husbands, brothers, fathers, and sons being murdered.

The most challenging interviews were those involving rape. We knew that many of these women had been gang raped, but it was very hard to get them to admit it, especially the young women. The cultural taboo was so great that it was considered better to be dead than raped. A woman who admitted being raped was abandoned by her husband, disowned by her father, cast out from the family. We tried to gently bring forth testimony so the rapists could be identified.

In the late afternoons, when we saw women gathering informally, Barbara Egenhauser and I would get sodas and snacks and, along with an interpreter, join their conversation. I'd always ask them their names and how old they were, and I was stunned to see the way suffering had aged them. Women in their forties looked twenty years older. When I looked into their eyes, I saw the same dazed, lost expressions, the hopelessness I had witnessed countless times in crime victims. It didn't matter that we spoke different languages. The universal language of the victim transcended every barrier.

In America, under the auspices of free speech, we allow our children to be exposed to murderous song lyrics and video games titled *Ethnic Cleansing*. We'd better wake up. We'd better decide how we're going to protect our values. Hate can find us, too. The children who play deadly games on their computers may be the next storm troopers. Or they may be the next victims.

CHAPTER 9

The Laws of Madness

To forgive is divine; but when it comes to violent criminals, I think we should leave the forgiving to God. Unfortunately, there's a tendency in this country, which often gets reflected in jury verdicts, to be too eager to find excuses for the defendant. Maybe it's too hard for people to face the terrible reality of evil. Whatever the reason, we long to find sensible explanations for even the most brutal of murders. Hearts bleed for the clean-cut young man looking so respectable in his courtroom attire. Surely he's a good boy gone astray. He's better now. Let's give him another chance. Before our eyes, in a perverse makeover, the murderer becomes the victim.

One of the greatest travesties in this rush to forgive and excuse is the use of the insanity defense. I have believed for a long time that the insanity defense has no place in a criminal trial. It should only be a consideration once the verdict is reached. In the fact-finding portion of the trial, the issue should be: Did he do it? Did he commit the crime? If he did, find him guilty. Convict him. Then deal with his mental illness at the sentencing phase. Insanity should not be used as an excuse for getting away with murder.

In my experience, the insanity defense, wrongly applied, does more to cause a loss of faith in the criminal justice system than any other issue. Nothing made that clearer to me than the shocking case of Michael Laudor.

In 1998, thirty-five-year-old Michael Laudor was the most famous schizophrenic in America. Most people had yet to hear of the brilliant Princeton mathematician John Nash, portrayed by the actor Russell Crowe in the Ron Howard film, *A Beautiful Mind.*

Laudor was the schizophrenic du jour, the poster boy for conquering the horrors of severe mental illness. He had graduated Yale University in three years, then Yale Law School. He was getting a tremendous amount of positive attention. It was Laudor who was profiled glowingly in *The New York Times* for having triumphed over his schizophrenia. It was Laudor who received a $600,000 advance from the publishing house Charles Scribner's Sons for a book focusing on his battle with the disease to be titled *Laws of Madness.* It was Laudor who was offered $1.5 million by Ron Howard's Imagine Entertainment to make his story the subject of a movie, potentially starring Brad Pitt. And it was Laudor who killed his fiancée, Carrie Costello, by stabbing her to death one afternoon in June 1998.

So many people were financially and emotionally invested in Laudor's ability, through medication, counseling, and sheer force of will, to control the mad demons of his disease, that his gradual deterioration went virtually unnoticed.

One person did know, however. Carrie Costello, thirty-seven, was the most important person in Michael Laudor's life. She saw him spiraling downward into madness, but she loved him and believed in him. She wasn't going to run away. It was another rough patch. They'd get through it together.

Carrie was a Yale graduate, and had a Master's degree from Harvard. She was associate director of technology at the Edison Project, a private company that managed public schools. Quiet, bright, and intensely devoted to Laudor, Carrie had nurtured him through his rocky times and accepted his mercurial temperament, which could be by turns brilliant or delusional.

The couple lived together in an apartment in the small town of Hastings-on-Hudson, New York, with sweeping views of the Hudson River. Everyone who knew them agreed that they were very much in love. They were planning their wedding.

On the morning of June 17, Carrie called her boss at Edison and said she wouldn't be able to make it into work that day because of a personal emergency. At some point during the day, Laudor's mother, Ruth, who lived a few miles away in New Rochelle, called the apartment. When Laudor answered the phone, Ruth asked to speak with Carrie. Laudor replied that she couldn't come to the phone because he had just killed her. Ruth called the Hastings police. The police later characterized her as distraught and fearful for the safety of her son and his fiancée.

Police went to the apartment where they found Carrie dead in a pool of blood on the kitchen floor. She had been stabbed repeatedly in the head, neck, and upper extremities with a pair of chef's knives. Michael was nowhere to be found.

Covered with Carrie's blood, Laudor had fled the carnage in her black Honda Civic, driving north to Binghamton, New York, where he abandoned the car and boarded a bus to Ithaca. He made his way to the campus of Cornell University. When he arrived there, he flagged down a college security patrol car and told the officer that he might have killed his girlfriend because she was going to have him sent away again.

Laudor was taken into custody and returned to Westchester County, where he was charged with second degree murder. Carrie's parents were called, and their sad journey began.

Families who lose one of their own to sudden, violent murder always have the same look about them—shell-

shocked, numb, their eyes distant and unfocused. I recognized the familiar demeanor when Carrie Costello's
parents were ushered into my office. They had just come
from the medical examiner, where they had viewed
their daughter's body. They had learned an additional
piece of news that deepened their torment. Carrie had
been one month pregnant. As I led them to chairs their
eyes drifted away. It was too painful to look at me and be
reminded of the reason they were there.

"Have you eaten?" I asked, because I suspected they
hadn't. They shook their heads no, so I asked my secretary
to order some sandwiches. The last thing they wanted to
do was eat, but I knew they would need their strength
for the ordeal ahead.

I sat across from them and in a quiet voice told them
what we believed had happened, sparing as many of the
gruesome details as I could. I didn't tell them the number of stab wounds. In time they would learn everything. If the case against Michael Laudor went to trial,
they would have to be prepared to see crime scene photos and hear the most graphic accounts of their daughter's murder detailed again and again.

"You need to focus on healing your family," I said.
"The burden of prosecution is mine. I will keep you informed every step of the way. I want you to call me any
time you have a question, no matter how small. I know
it's hard to believe right now, but your lives will someday be normal again. It will be a different normal than

before, but it will eventually happen." Even as I spoke, I knew that these good and decent people, who loved their daughter so much, would relive her killing again and again. The images, real and imagined, would haunt them for the rest of their lives.

As our investigation continued, I spoke to the Costellos on many occasions. I broke the painful news to them that we believed Laudor had been abusive to Carrie in the past. I told them we had learned that she was taking medication to handle the stress of living with a schizophrenic. It hurt them deeply to know that their daughter had carried this awful weight on her shoulders and they hadn't known anything about it. What hurt them the most was the way Carrie disappeared in the frenzy of public discussion about her famous killer. Nobody was talking about Carrie's hopes and dreams and ambitions. It was all about Michael Laudor. While the media focused on Michael Laudor's regrettable lapse into madness, the woman who had been his greatest supporter barely earned a line or two in the news reports.

Laudor's defenders began to construct a complex scaffold of excuses for him. Laudor had stopped taking his medications. The pressures of a book contract and movie deal had been too much for him. They claimed he was not responsible for his actions. He thought he was stabbing a doll, not his beloved Carrie. He said he heard voices. He didn't know what he was doing. He was insane. He shouldn't be held responsible.

I told Carrie's parents that I believed Michael Laudor was responsible for Carrie's murder and I was determined to have him held accountable.

Was Michael Laudor legally insane when he stabbed Carrie Costello to death? In medieval times, that would have been easy to figure out. Then, legal insanity was determined using the "Wild Beast Test." If the accused person behaved like a wild beast—growling, snarling, tearing his hair, soiling himself—he was declared legally insane.

By 1843 this standard was clearly inadequate. An attempt was made to understand the motivations of the accused. One such man was a Scottish woodcutter named Daniel M'Naghten, who went on trial in London for shooting and killing the prime minister's secretary. He acted under the belief that he was shooting the prime minister, who he thought was plotting against him. At trial his attorneys pleaded that he should be acquitted, because he was obviously insane and did not understand what he was doing. M'Naghten was acquitted and there was a huge uproar. Soon after, the House of Lords issued the following ruling:

> To establish a defense on the ground of insanity, it must clearly be proved that, at the time of the committing of the act, the party accused was laboring

under such a defect of reason, from disease of the
mind, as not to know the nature and quality of the
act he was doing; or if he did know it, that he did
not know what he was doing was wrong.

This ruling, which became known as the M'Naghten
Rule, was the legal standard for over a century. In the
United States today, about one-third of the states still
use a variation of the M'Naghten Rule. Six states have
modified the M'Naghten rule to add a reference to "ir-
resistible impulse," and two states, Montana and Idaho,
have abolished the insanity defense altogether. Those
found "guilty but mentally ill" are incarcerated in pris-
ons along with other convicts.

About half the states have adopted a test for the insanity defense written by the American Law Institute in
the 1950s, stating that a person would "not [be] responsible for criminal conduct if at the time of such conduct, as a result of mental disease or defect, he lacks
substantial capacity either to appreciate the criminality
of his conduct or to conform his conduct to the re-
quirements of law."

Was Lauder responsible for his actions? Schizophrenics are delusional, they hear voices, experience halluci-
nations, and hold false perceptions of reality. However,
several large studies support the fact that mentally ill
people are no more likely to commit violent acts than
anyone else. The MacArthur Violence Risk Assessment

Study, published in 1998, found that delusions did not predict a higher rate of violent behavior. Violence was more likely to be associated with extreme fits of anger and impulsiveness than it was with delusions.

Once the court ruled that Laudor was able to assist in his defense, the issue shifted to the question of guilt. Had Laudor possessed the intent necessary to be held responsible for Carrie's death?

I retained the services of Park Dietz, a forensic psychiatrist who had testified in high-profile cases. I liked Park, and I was impressed by his work. He interviewed Laudor and then called me on the phone.

"I have to conclude in my report that he was suffering from a mental disease defect at the time of the killing," Park told me apologetically.

"Damn." I shook my head in disgust.

"He thought Carrie was evil. In his mind, it's all about good and evil," Park mused.

"No, Park," I replied, "that's my mind you're talking about. In my mind it's all about good and evil, and Laudor is evil. He killed that girl."

The reports of the psychiatrists would win the day, effectively taking the matter out of the hands of the law. It was infuriating. The court accepted the opinions of the psychiatrists that Laudor was not responsible for his actions. Laudor was remanded to a psychiatric facility, where he remains to this day. His status is subject to review every two years. His book contract was canceled.

Ron Howard's Imagine Entertainment soon found another compelling schizophrenic to feature as the subject of a film biography.

There are millions of schizophrenics who function normally in society, who don't murder other people. Even assuming Michael Laudor didn't fully know what he was doing, Carrie's life mattered, and Laudor was responsible for taking it. There must be accountability.

The insanity defense is often misused, in my opinion, as a cover for rage, or in cases where there is no other defense. For example, the lawyers initially representing Colin Ferguson, the man who shot and killed six commuters on the Long Island Railroad in 1993, floated the "black rage" defense, claiming Ferguson was expressing an uncontrollable rage built on two hundred years of racial oppression.

The Menendez brothers, who murdered their parents in cold blood in California in 1989, used the "abuse excuse," saying they were so traumatized by past abuse that they were driven to kill to protect themselves from the possibility of further abuse. Neither of those defenses worked, but John Hinckley managed to convince a jury that he was legally insane when he tried to assassinate President Ronald Reagan in 1981 to impress the actress Jodie Foster. The Hinckley jury was instructed that the prosecution must prove his sanity beyond a reasonable doubt, but the defense had produced expert testimony to the contrary. Regardless of how much competing expert testimony the prosecution introduced, the very fact that some expert was willing to testify that Hinckley was insane was, in the jury's view, enough for reasonable doubt. He was acquitted and committed to a mental institution. He remains there, but has been allowed to go on supervised excursions to malls and bookstores.

Here's the problem: A trial searches for the truth. A psychiatrist searches for an explanation. The two are incompatible. A psychiatrist examines the defendant outside of a legal setting. The defendant is not subjected to the same cross-examination that a prosecutor would engage in to test the truth of his statement. He just tells his story, and then the psychiatrist goes off into his sanctum and issues an opinion. Usually, the defense hires a psychiatrist and the prosecution hires a psychiatrist. If they disagree, as they may do, the court or jury is treated to vying psychiatric conclusions and is supposed to decide which one is valid. If the psychiatrists agree that the defendant's untested tale is grounds for insanity, suddenly the case is yanked out of the criminal justice system, with all of its truth-testing mechanisms.

Essentially, we've taken a system designed to get at the truth through the presentation of evidence and testimony by sworn witnesses, and we've turned it into a trial by psychiatrist's report. The defendant is, in effect, "testifying" through the psychiatrist, but we can't cross-examine that testimony.

One example was the case of Paul Harnisch. Harnisch was an assistant district attorney, first in Manhattan, and then in Orange County, New York. He was well versed in the law, including the law on insanity. One of his final cases employed the insanity defense.

Harnisch suffered from bipolar disorder, and he experienced wide mood swings. He loved to drive fast. On Saturday, June 26, 1999, he was speeding near a shopping center and he sideswiped a car, knocking off the side mirror. Continuing along for another five miles, he turned off the road onto a bike path and challenged a boy on a bicycle to a race. He then sped off along the path, at a speed of forty-five to fifty miles per hour. Several hundred feet later, he slammed into a young newly-wed who was skating with his wife, killing him.

His car wrecked, Harnisch got out and fled on foot into town, where he stole a Mercedes. When police finally captured him, he immediately asked for a lawyer.

The incident happened in neighboring Orange County, and because Harnisch was an assistant district attorney there, my office handled the prosecution. When we charged Harnisch with Depraved-Indifference Murder, he pled insanity, claiming that he thought he was test driving a nuclear car and the bike path was a test track. He was examined by psychiatrists retained by both sides, and they all accepted his explanation and declared him not criminally responsible for his conduct.

My hands were tied. How could I rebut an insanity claim when even the prosecution's expert agreed with it? I was convinced that if we'd just been given the chance to cross-examine Harnisch on his test-track story, we could reveal it as a cunning lie. After all, Harnisch was driving recklessly before he ever reached the "test track." What "test driver" would challenge a cyclist to a race? Why flee, steal a Mercedes, and immediately ask for a lawyer when apprehended? I believed Harnisch knew he had killed a man, and he also knew exactly what he had to say to get away with it.

The law doesn't give me the chance to test the truth of tales like Harnisch's. Even if the case had gone to trial, he would never be required to tell his story and face cross-examination by a prosecutor. The psychiatrists would tell it for him. By allowing defendants to escape cross-examination in insanity cases, we leave it to psychiatrists to expose liars, and that's not their specialty—it's mine.

People ask, "Who would speed a car down a narrow bike path if he wasn't crazy?" Our world is full of thrill seekers: skydivers, daredevils, drag racers, and, yes, murderers. Are high-wire walkers insane? Are people who run with the bulls of Pamplona insane? Just because a person gets a thrill out of driving recklessly, it doesn't mean he's crazy. In my mind, Harnisch was criminally liable, but we could not bring him to justice. When are we going to stop making legal excuses for people who terrorize the population just because we can't imagine ourselves acting that way?

Ours is a system of laws, not a system of excuses. The integrity of the system demands that we not turn it over to psychiatrists, whose profession by its nature deals with ephemera, not facts. As long as we allow violent criminals to manipulate the system and take shelter in the insanity defense, they will find ways to avoid responsibility.

Every year the Costellos send me a Christmas card. They know that Michael Laudor might someday walk out of the psychiatric ward into the light of freedom. Their daughter Carrie will never see the light again.

It's hard for many to look a person in the eye and say, "You are evil. You are a destroyer of innocent lives." We find comfort in finding an explanation for an act of evil. We want to believe in redemption and are captivated by the idea of a murderer who mends his ways. That appeared to be the case with Paul Cox, an outwardly sweet-tempered young man with bright blue eyes and a pleasant, cherubic face.

Paul Cox was, in the parlance of Alcoholics Anonymous, a "recovering alcoholic." Good for him. There was just one problem: He was a killer. On New Year's Eve, 1988, when he was twenty years old, Cox was out and about, reeling around on a bad bender. Violently drunk, he broke into a home in Larchmont, the house where he had been raised. In the bedroom in which his mom and dad had slept, Paul Cox viciously attacked Lakshman Rao Chervu, fifty-eight, and his wife Shanta Chervu, fifty-one. The couple, both physicians, had bought the home from Cox's parents just a few years before. Cox would later say he thought he was stabbing his parents. Instead, he butchered two people he didn't even know.

The murder scene was gruesome. The Chervus' throats had been slit, and each had been stabbed at least ten times. For a long time no one knew who had murdered them. Their family was devastated. Their neighbors were terrified. Time passed without any clues. There were no leads, no motives. The crime remained unsolved for nearly four years.

It wasn't until Paul Cox began attending Alcoholics Anonymous meetings in the 1990s that the truth finally came out. Cox found a girlfriend, a fellow recovering alcoholic. He told her first. Then, after attending a meeting, Cox went out for coffee with some of his fellow members. It was there that he said he might have committed murder during an "alcoholic blackout" years before. He wasn't sure, but he might have. It was a compelling story. He ended up telling about seven or eight people, all AA members.

One of his friends from AA called the police. The police brought Cox in for questioning, and the Chervu double homicide case was suddenly solved. Bloody palm and fingerprint evidence preserved from the murder scene matched Cox's prints exactly. Cox told the cops he was in an alcoholic stupor when he broke into his childhood home. He had a blackout. He did not intend to kill the Chervus.

Cox first went to trial in 1994, and his defense was

temporary insanity brought on by alcohol-induced psychosis. We had to prove beyond a reasonable doubt that Cox was functioning on a rational level when he killed the Chervus and that he intended to commit murder. We knew that he was rational enough to go to a specific address with the intention of killing a person or persons. It doesn't matter that the people he killed were not the people he intended to kill. The intention to kill living, breathing human beings was there. Furthermore, the fact that Cox didn't remember committing the murders until several years later didn't necessarily mean that he wasn't conscious at the time he was doing it.

Even if we accepted that Paul Cox "blacked out" before breaking into his old home, or had no idea he viciously attacked and murdered two people, were we to believe that "alcohol-induced psychosis" was a reasonable excuse? In the same way that a drunk behind the wheel is guilty of vehicular homicide if someone dies at his hands, so is the drunk who breaks into your home guilty of assault and murder if he happens to kill you in the process.

Cox sat quietly at the defense table throughout the trial, his blandly handsome face cool and concerned. He was the boy next door, a blushing youth who had distanced himself from the terrible brutality of his crime. He barely reacted when the AA members to whom he'd confessed testified at his trial as witnesses for the prosecution. The evidence against him was incontrovertible;

yet, to look at him, the prosecutor might have been talking about someone else—Cox's "evil twin" perhaps, that alcoholic madman who had been put to rest long ago.

For the most part, the jury didn't buy the ruse, quickly reaching an initial vote of eleven in favor of conviction. There was one holdout, a young woman who insisted Paul Cox was not guilty. To this day, I believe that the holdout juror was simply enamored with Cox. She didn't have to give a reason. She simply refused to deliberate. The jury hung.

On March 14, 1995, we retried Paul Cox, now twenty-seven, before another jury. The second jury found him guilty on two counts of First-Degree Manslaughter, and he was given maximum consecutive terms of 16⅔ to 50 years.

The Chervu family was allowed to address the court prior to sentencing. They expressed the searing pain the death of their loved ones had caused them. Choking back tears, the Chervus' daughter, Aran Johnson, dismissed Cox's claims of temporary insanity as "psychological mumbo jumbo" and his recollections of his unhappy childhood as "the Twinkie defense."

Then Paul Cox addressed the court, breaking down in tears. I believe they were not for the Chervus, but for himself. The Chervus had been dead for more than six years when he was sentenced. Paul Cox had lived and breathed all that time, and now was being allowed to express his feelings of remorse.

Finally, he was led off to begin serving his prison sentence.

Cox appealed the conviction to the Appellate Court, and the conviction was upheld. He then went to the Court of Appeals, the highest court in New York, which saw no basis to review the case.

Once an appeals process has been exhausted, an individual has the right to petition a federal court for a writ of habeas corpus, alleging that he is in jail in violation of his constitutional rights. Cox's lawyers filed the writ.

I was in my office when the call came from ADA George Bolen. The District Court judge, sitting in White Plains, had overturned Paul Cox's conviction, thrown out his confessions and dismissed all charges against him. The judge ruled that the law considered AA a religion, and the Cox confession violated its promise of confidentiality. He ordered Cox's release, once prosecution appeals were exhausted.

When I learned of the judge's decision I almost fell over. In twenty-five years in law enforcement and on the bench, I had never dreamed that conversations between fellow alcoholics, who met through AA, would be equated with a priest-penitent confession or a psychiatrist-patient therapy session. The state legislature had not made it law, establishing a privilege for AA-type programs. The conversations in which Cox confessed to fellow AA members didn't even take place at a meeting, but in casual settings.

The Chervu family was shell-shocked. At a time when they were finally starting to put these devastating events behind them, they were being pulled back into the nightmare. You can understand why people get angry with the system. No wonder victims don't heal. Here it was, nearly fourteen years since the Chervus were murdered, and six years after their killer's conviction, and a judge could still dismiss the charges.

Of course the media loved it. What a terrific story. Paul Cox was a nice guy who went astray, but now he was back, repentant. Because the outside package didn't match the stereotype of a violent killer, Cox was given far too much attention and far more sympathy than he would have otherwise deserved. If he had looked like a thug, I suppose news shows wouldn't have devoted entire hours to exploring his case.

There was little interest in the messy killings of the Indian immigrant physicians. The news correspondents were more engaged in the back story, the cause of Paul Cox's pain. And then, of course, there was the aftermath. Was talking to fellow AA members like going to confession?

The Chervus were almost beside the point. Two innocent people—a doctor who specialized in nuclear medicine, and his doctor wife who specialized in geriatrics—had been butchered because of a young alcoholic's personal problem, having nothing whatsoever to do with them. Their only mistake had been to buy Paul Cox's childhood home.

The judge's decision was reversed by the U.S. Court of Appeals in Manhattan. Cox's lawyer petitioned the United States Supreme Court to hear the case.

On Monday, February 24, 2003, more than fifteen years after Lakshman Rao Chervu and his wife Shanta were murdered, the Supreme Court denied the appeal. At last the Chervus can rest in peace.

The mental health culture is based on making excuses, finding reasons for behavior that is plainly evil. The dead victims fade from view as their living killers don the mantle of victim or hide behind phony arguments that cloud the truth. If we turn our laws over to the psychiatrists, counselors and self-help gurus, they will, indeed, become laws of madness.

CHAPTER 10

In Memory

Kristie Bruen would have been about twenty-seven years old today. Instead, her life was snatched away at the tender age of four, when she was just beginning to become aware of the world around her. Kristie never got to experience the excitement of her first day of school. She never had the pleasure of going to movies with friends, or playing hopscotch on the sidewalk outside of her home. Kristie never went on a first date, never got to get all dressed up for her first prom. She didn't have an opportunity to dream of her future, travel, learn to drive, go to college, or work at something she loved. She never had a wedding day, or felt the joy of holding her own child.

Four-year-old Kristie's limp, battered body was brought to Peekskill Hospital at 10:40 P.M. on October 30, 1980, by her mother, Jana Bruen, and Jana's live-in boyfriend, Wesley Fisher. Kristie was pronounced dead on arrival from a massive brain clot. Emergency room doctors and nurses, all hardened professionals who'd seen a wide range of trauma, were aghast as they further examined Kristie. She was covered from head to toe with welts, burns, and bruises. When questioned, Jana Bruen and Wesley Fisher insisted she'd fallen down a flight of stairs. That was all.

Kristie's autopsy catalogued a more detailed history. Each bump and bruise was analyzed and dated. The medical examiner established a pattern of brutality that had been years in the making. Each cigarette burn on her buttocks was logged and its age identified. There had been no fall down any stairs the night of Kristie's death.

Like many victims, Kristie was speaking from the grave, her broken body revealing her tortured existence and providing the law with the means to bring her tormentors to justice. Confronted with the overwhelming evidence of their barbaric behavior, Jana Bruen and Wesley Fisher reluctantly admitted that the child may have been struck too hard while being punished. As Fisher explained it, the couple had devised a system of "reprimandation," meant to keep Kristie and her siblings—six-year-old twins, a brother and sister—in line. When the children broke any of the myriad rules, the adults would interrogate them, asking if they knew that what they did was wrong.

When the children said yes, they would be punished, usually with a large wooden paddle shaped like a cutting board. Often, they were denied food and water if they misbehaved. I'll never forget Jana's cold eyes and the hardened set of her face as she explained that Kristie was hardheaded.

"I'm not about to let that child walk all over me, which she'll do if you let her," she stated emphatically, her voice tight with anger as she spoke of her dead daughter in the present tense. "No one walks all over me, especially my kids." She denied burning Kristie's buttocks with lit cigarettes, saying that Kristie had a habit of backing into her cigarette. The night Kristie died, she was being punished for one infraction or another, and had been sent to bed without dinner. Desperately hungry, she snuck into the kitchen and took an open can of peas from the refrigerator. She was sitting on the kitchen floor, eating peas with her hands, when her mother found her.

As chief of the Domestic Violence Unit, I was involved in the case at the outset. Jana Bruen and Wesley Fisher were charged with First-Degree Manslaughter in Kristie's death. I would have liked to try the case, but at that time women were not assigned to homicide cases in Westchester County. The belief was that we weren't tough enough. It wasn't until 1983, eight years after I joined the DA's office, that I tried my first homicide. I got a conviction in that trial and in every murder trial I prosecuted after that.

Jana Bruen and Wesley Fisher were convicted and sent to prison, and Kristie's brother and sister disappeared into the foster care system. Life went on, but Kristie stayed on my mind. Her death affected me like no other, and I can't say why, exactly, except that it was so heartless and unfair. I found it especially poignant that Kristie's death occurred the night before Halloween, a time of such delight and anticipation for children. While other kids in the neighborhood were getting their costumes ready for trick-or-treating, and dreaming of the sweet treasures that would fill their Halloween bags, Kristie was being thrown against a wall, over and over again, until she died.

It bothered me that no one remained to mourn Kristie's passing, to remember her birthday, to bring flowers to her grave. Young children who are murdered by violent parents seem to leave this earth without a trace, unloved and forgotten. In her brief life, Kristie never experienced love, or warmth, or safety. In death, she would be nothing more than a statistic.

I made a commitment that Kristie and others like her would be more than just statistics. Five years after her death, when my first child was born, I named her after Kristie, as a gesture of respect and a prayer of hope. When I look at my bright, beautiful daughter, who is so dearly loved and so full of possibility, I see what every child deserves.

There is no typical victim of violent crime. Victims are young and old, rich and poor, men and women. They are well educated and unschooled, members of loving families and of dysfunctional families. They are any one of us. They are all of us.

There is no reliable precursor, no predictable timing for victimization. One minute, we are enjoying the bounties of life and fretting over the most inconsequential matters. The next minute, everything is different. Our worlds, and the worlds of everyone we loved and who loved us, are permanently branded with a life-shattering event. Sometimes there are warnings, but often there are none. We answer the door, we stop for a slice of pizza, we sign on to a Web site, we fall asleep in our beds at night, and suddenly we are a gruesome statistic.

It happens, and it will continue to happen. We can't really stop evil in its tracks—or can we? We can expose the truth. We can fight the system that coddles criminals. We can demand punishment for the predators and protection for their victims.

The greatest flaw of the criminal justice system is its fear of the truth. In a criminal trial, the horrors of violent crime are suppressed. The most shocking evidence is excluded. Photographs of victims, in the exact position their killers left them, lying in pools of their own blood, their eyes wide from a last moment of terror, are considered too emotional, too prejudicial, for juries to view. A victim's words—the desperate, unanswered pleas for help before the end—are excluded from trial testimony as hearsay.

In our system, the rights of the defendant are sacrosanct. The rights of the victim are marginalized. In New York, a defendant convicted of capital murder may stand before a judge and jury and plead for mercy, while the victim's loved ones cannot say a word about the wreckage he has made of their lives.

We who sit in the prosecutor's seat share in the deception. We are required to coach victims not to say too much, even when it's true. We must warn them not to give testimony that might be detrimental to the defendant's right to a fair trial, fearing a mistrial if they misspeak. We don't allow victims to tell the plain and simple truth, and yet we hire experts to explain in abstract terms what might have occurred.

The system expects us to be detached, dispassionate—but why? A person is dead, or injured, or damaged in ways we can't fully know. Others are coping with unfathomable loss. We simply aren't angry enough. We don't demand vengeance. Maybe it's because we can't face a more bitter truth—that tomorrow it could be any one of us lying in the morgue or sobbing at a gravesite. We may sense the true danger, but we hide from it by making distinctions between the victims and ourselves. If we can place the onus on the victim—"She should never have gotten involved with him . . . he should have known better than to drive through that neighborhood . . . he was drinking . . . she was dressed too provocatively . . ."— we can convince ourselves that the same fate could never befall us. After all, *we* wouldn't stay in a violent relationship. *We* wouldn't live with a schizophrenic. *We* wouldn't go jogging alone at night.

In the process of blaming the victim, we make the defendant less than a demon. We search for excuses for inexcusable behavior. We engage in what amounts to a therapy session for the defendant, casting his violence as society's failure, asking what caused his criminal behavior. While the victim is scrutinized for every wrong turn she may have taken in life, the defendant is analyzed with sympathy. It is as if we're saying, "Enough about the dead; let's attend to the living."

It's a natural human instinct to turn away from horror. Even when we feel outrage, the emotion doesn't linger. Time, like waves upon a rock, smooths the edges of our memories. But we must fight nature. We must hone our memories so we can bear witness with clarity and purpose.

We must be resolved to punish the criminal and protect the victim. We must understand that a criminal trial takes place because a tragedy occurred. It is not entertainment. It is not a sporting event, where points are given for clever diversions. It is not an abstract debate between two lawyers. It is—or should be—a search for the truth. If a defendant can sit through a trial, looking clean cut and respectable in his freshly pressed suit, why can't jurors see a picture of his victim throughout the trial? Might that be too human? Might it create an unseemly bond?

Every defense attorney knows that a subtle bond is created between a defendant and jurors during the course of a trial. Sitting together through tedious testimony, sharing experiences, a joke in the courtroom, can create the impression that the defendant is not so different from them. From that point, it's not such a leap to decide that this seemingly respectable person couldn't possibly have performed such a horrific act.

I'm not saying the defendant doesn't have the right to look his best in court. I'm only saying that the victim should have the same right—to be there in the courtroom, in person or in photographs, bearing witness to the crime. We don't need to sanitize the facts. To do so tips the scale against the person who paid the dearest price, and who never chose to be a victim in the first place.

Our job cannot end after the trial, even when there is a conviction. No longer can we engage in the charade that all is well once we lock up the criminal. I would like to see us bring the same level of attention and resources that we use to rehabilitate, educate, house, and feed criminals to the task of healing the victims and their families. Our actions would represent a declaration that in this, the most violent society in the Western world, accountability is the norm.

Our legal system is so consumed with criminals and their rights that even its name gives them top billing. We call it the CRIMINAL Justice System when it should be the VICTIMS' Justice System. We coddle criminals as if they were the violated, not the violators.

Our justice system is supposed to punish and protect, but too often we get it backward. We punish victims by denying their trauma, by making excuses for their brutalizers, and by refusing to give them a voice. We protect criminals by creating rules of evidence that hide the truth, by cloaking them in respectability, and by finding fault with their victims. It's a screwed-up system.

The great judge Learned Hand once wrote, "The spirit of liberty remembers that not even a sparrow falls to earth unheeded." Liberty and justice cannot exist in a nation that is blind to its fallen victims—no matter how small their lives. It's hard to hear their voices above the cacophony of defense for their victimizers, but we'd better try, because any one of us could be a victim.

I think of the first time in Westchester County that a rape victim addressed the court prior to sentencing. The victim was a nurse who took an early bus to work her shift at a local hospital. The perpetrator confronted her at the bus stop. The brutal rape left her devastated. She told the judge that for weeks after the attack she couldn't leave her home, and she was afraid to be alone at night. She said that she saw her own body as something vile and repulsive. As she spoke, it was clear that this seasoned judge, who had presided at the trial, was just then, for the first time, realizing the depth of the destruction the defendant had unleashed on her.

Jurors hear none of this, even when a victim testifies. These very real consequences of criminal conduct are considered too prejudicial for a victim to fully recount at trial. Who are we trying to kid? By keeping the reality of crime at bay we believe that justice is somehow served. We separate ourselves rather than engage the victims. When we listen to them at all it is after a verdict has been rendered.

Justice is not only something we deliver *to* the criminal. It should also be something we do *for* the victim. But, as this example illustrates, even experienced judges don't truly understand what victims endure. Judges are provided with stacks of official information about defendants; they receive only selected bits about victims. How can victims assume their rightful place in our priorities when decision makers know so little about them?

This is my world. This is my fight and my cause. I want our system to hear these voices. I want us to remember and to act, to bear responsibility and not make excuses. I want our system to hold criminals accountable while giving equal attention to finding justice for their victims.

I remember Patricia Torres and her innocent children, Debbie Safian, Janet Petit, Diane Smith, Renee Linton, Anne Scripps Douglas, Daniel C., Connie Rogers, Mary

Rogers, Margaret Raffaele, Charles Guardino, Alberto Reyes, O. Winston Link, Margaret Brigham, Charles Campbell, Carrie Costello, Lakshman and Shanta Chervu, and Kristie Bruen. I remember their faces, mostly from autopsy photographs, their eyes reflecting the horror of their final moments. I remember others, such as Janet Petit and Renee Linton, as they were in life. They lived among us in constant fear that their abusers would finally fulfill their promises to kill them. We watched silently, unable or unwilling to offer meaningful protection, as their fears were realized.

Now Kristie and Janet and all the others stand as silent witnesses, waiting to see if we will find the will and the courage to assure their suffering was not in vain.

APPENDIX A
_____

Westchester County District Attorney's Crime Prevention Programs

During my tenure as DA, I've been proactive in finding and developing programs that empower citizens and fight crime. The following are extremely effective. If law enforcement in your community isn't engaged in similar efforts, demand that they become more proactive. The citizenry deserves no less.

CLEAR CHOICES
**Substance Abuse Prevention
for Middle School Students**

Clear Choices is an award-winning aggressive, peer-driven, community-based, substance abuse prevention program for middle school children, which I developed in 1997. Clear Choices places strong emphasis on parental involvement. The program is specifically designed to strengthen the families of middle schoolers and assist them in the development of positive attitudes toward the prevention of drug and alcohol abuse. The focus of the program is not only on the students but on the parents.

Research indicates that there is a "window of opportunity" of thirty-six months between the beginning of sixth grade and the end of ninth grade when young people are at the most risk of being introduced to drugs and/or alcohol. If a child reaches the age of fifteen without using drugs/alcohol, he or she is less likely to have a problem with those substances as a young adult. Clear Choices seeks to achieve that result.

The Task Force is comprised of a member of the Westchester County District Attorney's Office, a representative from the Center for Human Options, Inc. (a New York State certified drug prevention agency), a member of NND Productions, Inc. (an adolescent substance abuse consultant firm), a representative from the Cornerstone Treatment Facilities Network, a representative from the Westchester Medical Center, a representative from the National Council on Alcoholism and Drug Dependence (NCADD), and members of the middle school. The Task Force is responsible for the day-to-day operation of the program, which includes four interactive workshops by professionals in the fields of law, physical and mental health, and substance abuse prevention. Peer leadership training and a peer co-counseling room are also employed.

WATCHFUL EYE
A Home Security Program for Senior Citizens

One half of all crime victims sixty-five years or older are victimized at or near their homes. Senior citizens are often targeted by criminals motivated by economic gain. Criminals prey on seniors because they are perceived to be more vulnerable than younger victims. I developed the Watchful Eye program to help seniors take steps to better protect themselves.

Watchful Eye provides senior citizens, free of charge, with the installation of wide-angled peepholes in the entrance ways of their houses and apartments. This simple step insures that uninvited visitors are not allowed into their homes. In addition, the program provides seniors with a portable air horn to sound in case of an emergency. Assistant district attorneys sit down with seniors and advise them on how to prevent push-in crimes.

OPERATION SAFE SMILES
An Identification "Passport" for Child Protection

Operation Safe Smiles is a countywide child identification program, a program aimed at protecting Westchester's most valuable resource: its children. Initiated by my office in 1994, the bilingual program (Spanish and English) provides children between the ages of two and twelve, at no cost, with a complete identification "passport" containing each child's color photograph, fingerprints, and personal information, including height, weight, and identifying features. Unlike most child-identification kits, Safe Smiles allows parents to update the photographs as children get older.

The ID passports, once assembled, are given to parents and guardians to maintain should their child ever become lost or missing. In case of an emergency, the passports can be turned over to police departments to facilitate the speedy recovery of lost or missing children. No identification information is maintained by the local police or the District Attorney's office. Quite simply, the parents or guardians of children are the best caretakers of this personal information.

To date, over forty-five thousand children in Westchester County have been provided with identification passports at hundreds of sites throughout the county. Our office works in conjunction with local police departments in Westchester County to insure that this important and free program is available to all of Westchester's children. More than one hundred members of my staff, along with local police departments, provide the volunteer effort required to photograph, weigh, measure, and fingerprint each of the participants.

Pro-Law
Prosecutors Reach Out Legal Awareness Workshops
for High School Students

I created PRO-LAW to educate high school students about the law and criminal conduct, which may affect them in their daily lives. The topics range from date rape to bias crimes, alcohol and drug abuse to youth gangs, weapon possession to computer crimes. Assistant district attorneys "adopt" a school, preferably one in a municipality where they currently reside or one they had attended. This is done to establish a connection between the community and my office. It also promotes familiarity between the students and the assistant district attorneys, to create an open line of communication.

There are six PRO-LAW workshops:

· Violence—At Home, At School, and on the Streets
· Drugs, Alcohol, and Gambling—Three Ways to Ruin Your Life
· Date Rape and Other Sexual Abuse
· Busted
· www.crime.com—Crime and the Internet
· Teen Pranks

Since its inception, PRO-LAW has been used by fifty public and private schools in Westchester County.

CRASH COURSE
A Drunk Driving Reality Program
for High School Students

My office joined with the Nurses Network of America. NNA has a program called Crash Course, which employs a mobile emergency room and depicts a DWI accident involving students where a fatality occurs. This program has great shock value as it brings home the physical as well as the emotional injuries teenagers can sustain when they drive drunk or are a passenger in a car driven by a drunk driver. An assistant district attorney then speaks to the students about the legal consequences they face when they get involved with alcohol and are underage. The assistant district attorney focuses on DWI, the use of fake identification to gain entrance to bars and "house parties."

WESTCHESTER CRIME STOPPERS
Engaging Citizens in the Fight Against Crime

Crime Stoppers is an international organization that I brought to Westchester County as a nonprofit organization. It involves a three-pronged effort of community, law enforcement, and the media working together in the fight against crime. It works through a reward system. Anyone who calls the 1-800-TIPS Hotline about a crime or the whereabouts of a fugitive is given a code number. Callers do not have to tell who they are—just what they know. If the information given results in an arrest, the caller is eligible to receive a cash reward of up to $5,000. The 1-800-TIPS Hotline is answered on a 24-hour basis. A board of volunteer citizens oversees Westchester Crime Stoppers and approves the rewards to be paid; however, this board never learns the identity of the caller.

ELDER ABUSE INITIATIVE
Educating and Protecting the Elderly

The Elder Abuse Initiative was jointly developed by my office with the Hebrew Home for the Aged at Riverdale. This program began as an educational vehicle for the elderly, law enforcement, civil service workers, and the general public to learn about the often invisible crimes perpetrated against older people. Our goal was to raise awareness of the financial exploitation, neglect, and physical violence that can victimize the most frail and defenseless seniors. My office and the Hebrew Home for the Aged at Riverdale held numerous seminars and training sessions, and even produced a palm card for law enforcement officers to carry while on duty. The increased awareness of the issue among professionals and the public has made our seniors safer, and has also resulted in subsequent arrests and prosecutions of elder abusers in our community.

WATCH YOUR CAR
Preventing Car Theft

This is a New York State Police program that I brought to Westchester County. This vehicle security program features free etching of Vehicle Identification Numbers (VIN) on automobile glass panels. Vehicles outfitted with etched glass are undesirable to "chop shops" since the glass becomes permanently linked to a particular vehicle, thus allowing police to identify the true owner if the vehicle is stolen.

APPENDIX B

Internet Safety: What Every Parent Should Know

These guidelines for Internet safety, developed by my office, are crucial for every parent. We must be proactive in keeping our children safe from Internet predators.

1. Be aware of what your children are doing on-line.

Don't be afraid to become involved. At home, set up your computer in the family room, den, or kitchen instead of a child's bedroom so that you can watch and learn what children are doing on-line. Periodically monitor their activities.

2. **Teach your children the fundamental rules for Internet use.**

Children are told not to talk to strangers, but are they told not to arrange to meet anyone that they have contacted via the Internet? A child should know not to give out personal information (name, home address, phone number, school name, or on-line password) via the Internet. They should be told never to accept electronic information on-line from strangers (like e-mail, files, or Web addresses). Some of these files contain graphic images or hidden programs that can damage a computer's hard drive or access confidential on-line account information.

3. **Warn your children never to chat with strangers on-line unless you are there to supervise.**

Ensure that your children access only chat rooms appropriate for their age group. Remind them that if someone says something that makes them feel uncomfortable they should not respond and should tell you immediately. Remember, there is no certainty that another Internet user is the person he or she claims to be. It is not unusual for individuals with criminal intent to assume a false identity.

4. **Protect your passwords.**

Don't allow younger children to log on by themselves. Do it for them to guard against the password becoming public.

5. **Screen what your child can access on the Internet.**

Screening software will protect children from offensive, inappropriate, or dangerous materials. Check with your Internet or on-line service provider for information about the availability of screening software.

6. **Do not allow your children to have on-line profiles.**

An on-line profile is a brief description of an Internet user, including hobbies, nicknames, and so on. These profiles can be used by pedophiles to locate and identify potential victims. Even the most innocent profiles can reveal more information than intended.

Know the Facts About Crime: Are You at Risk?

An informed public is a safer public. Following is a compilation of crucial statistical information compiled by national agencies. It covers the issues discussed in this book, including domestic violence, child abuse, Internet pedophilia, underage drinking, elder crime and victimization, and hate crimes. There is also an overview that details general crime statistics. These analyses can provide data to help organizations, teachers, parents, and individuals in their efforts to keep our communities and families safe.

OVERVIEW: CRIME AND VICTIMIZATION

• In 2001 there were an estimated 24.2 million criminal victimizations. (Bureau of Justice Statistics, September 2002)

• In 2001 there were an estimated 18.3 million property crimes, including burglary, motor vehicle theft, and theft. There were an estimated 5.7 million violent crimes, including rape, sexual assault, robbery, aggravated assault and simple assault. (Ibid.)

• There were an estimated 248,000 rapes, attempted rapes, and sexual assaults in 2001. (Ibid.)

• Youths between the ages of 12 and 19 experience the highest rate of violent victimization in the United States, at a rate of 55 per 1,000 persons in the population. (Ibid.)

• Blacks experienced more violent assaults in 2001 than whites or persons of other races. Rates of rape and sexual assault, however, had similar incidence rates among blacks, whites, and persons of other races in 2001. (Ibid.)

• Hispanics were victims of violence at higher rates than non-Hispanics. Hispanics were robbery victims in 2001 at significantly higher rates: 5.3 per 1,000 persons compared to 2.4 per 1,000 for non-Hispanics. (Ibid.)

• Fifty percent of the violent victimizations recorded by the National Crime Victimization Survey were reported to the police in 2001, and 37 percent of the property crimes were reported to the police. (Ibid.)

• In 2001 crimes against female victims were more

likely to be reported to the police than crimes against male victims. Crimes against black female victims were 58 percent likely to be reported to the police, while crimes against white female victims were reported to the police 53 percent of the time. Crimes against female victims of other races were reported to the police 40 percent of the time. (Ibid.)

• There were 15,980 murders reported in 2001, reflecting a 2.5 percent increase over 2000. This figure does not include the terrorist attacks of September 11th. (Federal Bureau of Investigation, 2002)

• Firearms were used in 63.4 percent of the homicides committed in 2001. Knives were used in 13.1 percent of the homicides, other weapons in 16.8 percent of the homicides, and hands and feet were used in 6.7 percent of the homicides. (Ibid.)

DOMESTIC VIOLENCE: SPOUSE/PARTNER ABUSE

• More than 1.5 million women are physically and/or sexually abused by an intimate partner each year in the United States. (U.S. Department of Justice, 2000)

• Young women between the ages of 16 and 24 experience the highest rates of violence by current or former intimate partners. (Ibid.)

• Forty percent of teenage girls between the ages of 14 and 17 report knowing someone their age who has been hit or beaten by a boyfriend. (Children Now and Kaiser Permanente Poll)

• Three out of every four victims of violence are girls. (U.S. Department of Justice)

• Nearly one in every three adult women experiences at least one physical assault by a partner during adulthood. (American Psychological Association)

• Women who were physically assaulted by an intimate partner averaged 6.9 physical assaults by the same partner. (National Institute of Justice and the Centers for Disease Control and Prevention)

• Uniform Crime Reports from the Department of Justice indicate that females are ten times more likely to be killed by an intimate partner than are males.

CHILD ABUSE AND VICTIMIZATION

• In 1999, there were 67,000 runaway or thrown-away episodes among youth between the ages of 7 to 11 years old, many of whom were in danger because of the risk of sexual exploitation, criminal activity taking place in the area where they had "run" to, their extremely young age, and/or the risk of physical or sexual abuse when they returned home. (National Incidence Studies of Missing, Runaway, and Thrownaway Children, October 2002)

• Of the approximately 879,000 children found to be victims of child maltreatment in 2000, 63 percent were neglected, including medically neglected; 19 percent were physically abused; 10 percent were sexually abused; and 8 percent were psychologically maltreated.

(Children's Bureau, Administration of Children, Youth, and Families, April 2002)

• Approximately 1,200 children died of abuse or neglect in 2000, at a rate of 1.71 children per 100,000 children in the population. Forty-four percent of the children who died from abuse were under one year of age, and 85 percent of the children were younger than 6 years of age. (Ibid.)

• Victimization rates for male and female children in 2000 were similar in every category except for sexual abuse, where the rate for females was higher. There were 1.7 victims sexually abused per 1,000 female children and 0.4 victims sexually abused per 1,000 male children. (Ibid.)

• Parents were the perpetrators in 84 percent of the reported cases of child abuse in 2000. (Ibid.)

• Research into nonfamily child abductions found that in 1999 58,200 children were forced by a nonfamily perpetrator to go to an isolated place without parental permission for a substantial period of time. Forty percent of the children were threatened with a weapon, 46 percent were sexually assaulted, 31 percent were physically assaulted, 7 percent were robbed, and 4 percent were held for ransom. (National Incidence Studies of Missing, Runaway, and Thrownaway Children, October 2002)

CYBER CRIME AGAINST CHILDREN

· The Cyber Tipline at the National Center for Missing and Exploited Children received over 40,000 reports
of on-line sexually exploitative behavior directed at children between July 1998 and June 2001. During this period there were 192 reports of cyber-contact involving
child pornography, 4,026 reports of on-line enticement,
1,880 reports of child sexual molestation, 779 reports of
child prostitution, and 426 reports of child sex exploitation. (Office of Juvenile Justice and Delinquency Prevention, January 2002)

· One in five children between the ages of 10 and 17
will receive a sexual solicitation over the Internet each
year, and one in 33 will receive an aggressive invitation
to meet the solicitor, have telephone contact, or receive
mail, money, and gifts. (The National Center for Missing and Exploited Children, 2000)

· Of the 353 cyberstalking cases surveyed by Working to Halt Online Abuse (WHO@) in 2000, 39.5 percent began as e-mail communications, 15.5 percent as
chat room exchange, 13 percent from instant messaging,
9 percent from a Web-based message board, 8.5 percent
in a newsroom, 7 percent in a general Web site, 3 percent with a computer virus attack, and the rest were
miscellaneous contacts. (Working to Halt Online Abuse
[WHO@], 2002)

Underage Drinking

• Parents' drinking behavior, and favorable attitudes about drinking have been positively associated with adolescents' initiating and continuing drinking. (NIAAA, 1997)

• An early age of drinking onset is associated with alcohol-related violence not only among persons under age 21 but among adults as well. (Hingson et al., October 2001)

• Research continues to show that young drivers are more often involved in alcohol-related crashes than any other comparable age group. Alcohol-crash involvement rates and alcohol-crash risk are highest with young drivers, with the peaks for fatal crashes occurring at age 21. (NHTSA, 2001)

• The highest prevalence of both binge and heavy drinking in 2000 was for young adults aged 18 to 25, with the peak rate occurring at age 21. (SAMHSA 2000)

• Sixty-nine percent of young drivers (15–20 years old) of passenger vehicles involved in fatal crashes who had been drinking were not wearing seat belts. Of the young drivers who had been drinking and were killed, 80 percent were unrestrained. (NHTSA, 2000)

• One in ten American teenagers (22.3 million persons) drove under the influence of alcohol at least once in the 12 months prior to an interview in 2000 for a nationwide survey. (SAMHSA, 2000)

• Each year, college students spend approximately

$5.5 billion on alcohol—more than they spend on soft drinks, milk, juice, tea, coffee, and books combined. (Drug Strategies, 1999)

• Teenagers are not well informed about alcohol's effects. Nearly one-third of the teens responding to a 1998 American Academy of Pediatrics survey mistakenly believed that a 12-ounce can of beer contains less alcohol than a standard shot of distilled spirits. (Ibid.)

• Approximately one-fifth (20.6 percent) of persons aged 12 years and older (46 million people) participated in binge drinking at least once in 30 days prior to an alcohol use survey in 2000. This represents approximately 4 percent of all current drinkers. (SAMHSA, 2000)

• About 9.7 million persons aged 12 to 20 reported drinking alcohol in the month prior to a nationwide survey in 2000. Of these, 6.6 million were binge drinkers and 2.1 million were heavy drinkers. (Ibid.)

• Thirty percent of 15–20-year-old drivers killed in motor vehicle crashes during 2000 had been drinking. Twenty-one percent were intoxicated. (NHTSA, 2000)

• In 2001 approximately 2 in 5 (44.4 percent) of college students reported binge drinking, according to a college survey. This percentage is almost identical to rates in three previous surveys. (Weschsler et al., 2002)

• The median age at which children begin drinking is 13. Young people who begin drinking before age 15 are four times more likely to develop alcohol dependence than those who begin drinking at age 21. (CADCA, 1996)

• Students who attended schools with high rates of

heavy drinking experienced a greater number of second-hand effects, including disruption of sleep or studies, property damage, and verbal, physical, or sexual violence. (Weschsler et al., 2002)

• Binge drinking has been defined as at least five drinks in a row for men and four drinks in a row for women. (Ibid.)

• For ages 13–19, 53 percent of deaths in auto accidents were drivers, 47 percent were passengers. Based only on the driving age population 16–19, 60 percent were drivers, 40 percent were passengers. At ages 13–15, more young people were killed as passengers than as drivers. (IIHS, December 2001)

• Based on the latest mortality data available (1998), motor vehicle crashes are the leading cause of death for people from 15 to 20 years old. (NHTSA, 2000)

• The total cost attributable to the consequences of underage drinking was more than $58 billion per year in 1998 dollars. (Pacific Institute for Research and Evaluation, 1999)

• More than 40 percent of individuals who start drinking before the age of 13 will develop alcohol abuse or alcohol dependence at some point in their lives. (Grant, B. F. et al., 1997)

• Twenty-six percent of young male drivers involved in fatal crashes in 2000 had been drinking at the time of the crash, compared with 13 percent of the young female drivers involved in fatal crashes. (NHTSA, 2000)

ELDER CRIME AND VICTIMIZATION

· There were 846 homicides reported in 2001 of people 60 years of age and over. (Federal Bureau of Investigation, 2002)

· According to the National Crime Victimization Survey, there were 3.2 victimizations per 1,000 persons among individuals 65 years of age and older in 2001. (Bureau of Justice Statistics, September 2002)

· The proportion of individuals losing at least $5,000 in Internet frauds is higher for victims 60 years and older than it is for any other age category. (Federal Bureau of Investigation, 2002. *2001 Internet Fraud Report,* Washington, DC, U.S. Department of Justice)

· More than 25 percent of all the people who reported telemarketing frauds to the National Fraud Information Center during the first six months of 2002 were age 60 years and older. (National Fraud Information Center, August 2002)

· The top three telemarketing frauds against seniors are: magazine sales, for which the average loss is $98; credit card protection plans, for which the average loss is $229; and sweepstakes and prize offers, for which the average individual consumer loss is $2,752. (Ibid.)

· Between the years 1992–1997 the elderly were victims of 2.7 million property and violent crimes, 2.5 million household burglaries, motor vehicle thefts, and household thefts, 46,000 purse snatchings and pocket pickings, and 165,000 nonlethal violent crimes, including rape, robbery, and aggravated and simple assault. (Bureau of Justice Statistics, 2000)

· Neglect of the elderly is the most frequent type of maltreatment, and represents 48.7 percent of the abuse reported to adult protective services. (National Center on Elder Abuse, 1998)

· Emotional and psychological abuse are the second-most-reported elder abuse, followed by physical abuse. Thirty-five percent of elder abuse reported to adult protective services is emotional and psychological abuse, and 25 percent are reports of physical abuse. (Ibid.)

· Thirty percent of the elder abuse reported to adult protective services involves financial exploitation. Abandonment is the least-reported form of elder abuse. (Ibid.)

· For every incident of elder abuse reported, at least five go unreported. (The Administration on Aging, 1998)

HATE AND BIAS CRIMES

· In 2001, 9,726 incidents of hate and bias crime were reported to the FBI, involving 11,447 separate offenses, 12,016 victims, and 9,231 known offenders. (Federal Bureau of Investigation, 2002)

· Of the 9,726 incidents of hate and bias reported to the FBI, 44.9 percent were of racial bias, 21.5 percent were bias based on ethnicity or nationality; 18.8 percent were bias based on religious preference, and 14.3 percent were for sexual orientation. Intimidation is the most frequent kind of hate bias crime, followed by destruction of property. (Ibid.)

· The majority of perpetrators of hate and bias crime are white (65.5 percent) followed by African-American (20.4 percent). The remainder are of other races, mixed race, or their race is unknown. (Ibid.)

· Twelve percent of students between the ages of 12 and 18 reported that they had received hate-related insults at school during the 6 months prior to a 2001 survey. Insults included comments about their race, religion, ethnicity, disability, gender, and/or sexual orientation. (Bureau of Justice Statistics, November 2002)

· The National Coalition of Antiviolence Programs received reports of 11 lesbian, gay, bisexual, and transgender hate and bias murders, 82 rapes and sexual assaults, 732 assaults, 82 robberies, 141 acts of vandalism, 737 intimidations, and 1,142 verbal harassments. (Ibid.)

· There has been a 1,700 percent increase in reported hate and bias crimes against Arabs, Muslims, and those perceived to be Arab or Muslim, since the events of September 11, 2001. (Human Rights Watch, November 2002)

· At least 3 individuals were murdered after September 11 as a result of anti-Arab backlash. Four additional murders were suspected of being linked to the backlash. (Ibid.)

· Within 6 months of the events of September 11, the American-Arab Anti-Discrimination Committee (ADC) had received reports of 600 violent incidents di-

rected against Arab-Americans in the United States, including acts of physical violence, vandalism, arson, beatings, assault with weapons, and direct threats of specific
acts of violence. (American-Arab Anti-Discrimination
Committee, March 2002)

Milestones in Victims' Rights

The progress of victims' rights programs and legislation over the last forty years has amounted to substantive changes in the way victims are treated in the courts and in civil venues. These efforts, the work of thousands of citizens in local communities across the country, offer hope that victims will one day have a full voice.

1965

The first crime victim compensation program is established in California.

1972

The first three victim assistance programs are created.

1974

The first law enforcement–based victim assistance programs are established in Fort Lauderdale, Florida and Indianapolis, Indiana.

The U.S. Congress passes the Child Abuse Prevention and Treatment Act which establishes the National Center on Child Abuse and Neglect.

Citizen activists from across the country unite to expand victim services and increase recognition of victims' rights through the formation of the National Organization for Victim Assistance (NOVA).

1977

The National Association of Crime Victim Compensation Boards is established by the existing twenty-two compensation programs to promote the creation of a nationwide network of compensation programs.

1978

The National Coalition Against Sexual Assault (NCASA) is formed to combat sexual violence and promote services for rape victims.

The National Coalition Against Domestic Violence (NCADV) is organized as a voice for the battered women's movement on a national level.

Parents of Murdered Children, a self-help support group, is founded in Cincinnati, Ohio.

1979

Frank G. Carrington founds the Crime Victims' Legal
Advocacy Institute, Inc., to promote the rights of
crime victims in the civil and criminal justice systems.
(The nonprofit organization is renamed VALOR, the
Victims' Assistance Legal Organization, Inc., in 1981.)
The Office on Domestic Violence is established in the
U.S. Department of Health and Human Services, but
is later closed in 1981.

1980

Mothers Against Drunk Driving (MADD) is founded
after the death of thirteen-year-old Cari Lightner,
who was killed by a drunk driver who had prior drunk
driving arrests.
The U.S. Congress passes the Parental Kidnapping Prevention Act of 1980.
Wisconsin passes the first "Crime Victims' Bill of
Rights."

1981

The President proclaims "Crime Victims' Rights Week"
in April.

1982

The Federal Victim and Witness Protection Act of 1982
brings "fair treatment standards" to victims and witnesses in the federal criminal justice system.

California voters overwhelmingly pass Proposition 8, which guarantees restitution and other statutory reforms to crime victims.

The passage of the Missing Children's Act of 1982 helps parents guarantee that identifying information about their missing child is promptly entered into the FBI National Crime Information Center (NCIC) computer system.

1983

The Office for Victims of Crime (OVC) is created by the U.S. Department of Justice.

Wisconsin passes the first "Child Victim and Witness Bill of Rights."

1984

The passage of the Victims of Crime Act (VOCA) establishes the Crime Victims Fund, made up of federal criminal fines, penalties, and bond forfeitures, to support state victim compensation and local victim service programs.

The President signs the Justice Assistance Act, which establishes a financial assistance program for state and local government and funds two hundred new victim service programs.

The National Center for Missing and Exploited Children (NCMEC) is created as the national resource agency for missing children.

The U.S. Congress passes the Family Violence Prevention and Services Act, which earmarks federal funding for programs serving victims of domestic violence.

The Office for Victims of Crime establishes the National Victims' Resource Center, now named the Office for Victims of Crime Resource Center (OVCRC), to serve as a clearinghouse for OVC publications and other resource information.

1985

The National Victim Center (renamed in 1998 The National Center for Victims of Crime) is founded in honor of Sunny von Bulow to promote the rights and needs of crime victims, and to educate Americans about the devastating effect of crime on our society.

1988

The National Aging Resource Center on Elder Abuse (NARCEA) is established in a cooperative agreement among the American Public Welfare Association, the National Association of State Units on Aging, and the University of Delaware. Renamed the National Center on Elder Abuse, it continues to provide information and statistics.

The Federal Drunk Driving Prevention Act is passed, and states raise the minimum drinking age to twenty-one.

1990

The U.S. Congress passes the Hate Crime Statistics Act, requiring the U.S. Attorney General to collect data of incidence of certain crimes motivated by prejudice based on race, religion, sexual orientation, or ethnicity.

The Victims of Child Abuse Act of 1990, which features reforms to make the federal criminal justice system less traumatic for child victims and witnesses, is passed by the U.S. Congress.

The Victims' Rights and Restitution Act of 1990 incorporates a Bill of Rights for federal crime victims and codifies services that should be available to victims of crime.

U.S. Congress passes legislation proposed by MADD to prevent drunk drivers and other offenders from filing bankruptcy to avoid paying criminal restitution or civil fines.

The National Child Search Assistance Act requires law enforcement to enter reports of missing children and unidentified persons in the NCIC computer.

1991

U.S. Representative Ilena Ros-Lehtinen (R-FL) files the first Congressional Joint Resolution to place victims' rights in the U.S. Constitution.

The Violence Against Women Act of 1991 is considered by the U.S. Congress.

1992

The Battered Women's Testimony Act, which urges states to accept expert testimony in criminal cases involving battered women, is passed by Congress and signed into law by President Bush.

Twenty-eight states pass antistalking legislation.

1993

The President signs the "Brady Bill" requiring a waiting period for the purchase of handguns.

Congress passes the Child Sexual Abuse Registry Act, establishing a national repository for information on child sex offenders.

Twenty-two states pass antistalking statutes, bringing the total number of states with antistalking laws to fifty, plus the District of Columbia.

1994

Six additional states pass constitutional amendments for victims' rights—the largest number ever in a single year—bringing the total number of states with amendments to twenty. States with new amendments include Alabama, Alaska, Idaho, Maryland, Ohio, and Utah.

The President signs a comprehensive package of federal victims' rights legislation as part of the Violent Crime Control and Law Enforcement Act.

1995

The National Victims' Constitutional Amendment Network proposes the first draft of language for a federal constitutional amendment for victims' rights.

1996

Federal victims' rights constitutional amendments are introduced in both houses of Congress with bipartisan support.

Eight states ratify the passage of constitutional amendments for victims' rights—raising the total number of state constitutional amendments to twenty-nine nationwide.

The Community Notification Act, known as "Megan's Law," provides for notifying communities of the location of convicted sex offenders by amendment to the national Child Sexual Abuse Registry legislation.

The President signs the Antiterrorism and Effective Death Penalty Act, providing one million dollars in funding to strengthen antiterrorism efforts, making restitution mandatory in violent crime cases, and expanding the compensation and assistance services for victims of terrorism both at home and abroad, including victims in the military.

The Mandatory Victims' Restitution Act, enacted as Title II of the Antiterrorism and Effective Death Penalty Act, allows federal courts to award "public harm" restitution directly to state VOCA victim assistance programs.

The National Domestic Violence Hotline is established to provide crisis intervention information and referrals to victims of domestic violence and their friends and family.

The Drug-Induced Rape Prevention Act is enacted to address the emerging issue of drug-facilitated rape and sexual assault.

1997

In January, a federal victims' rights constitutional amendment is reintroduced in the opening days of the 105th Congress with strong bipartisan support.

In March, Congress passes at historic speed the Victims' Rights Clarification Act of 1997 to clarify existing federal law allowing victims to attend a trial and to appear as "impact witnesses" during the sentencing phase of both capital and noncapital cases. Supported by the Justice Department, the President immediately signs the Act, allowing the victims and survivors of the bombing of the Alfred P. Murrah Federal Building in Oklahoma City to both observe the trial that is scheduled to begin within days and to provide input later at sentencing.

In April, the Senate Judiciary Committee conducts hearings on the proposed federal constitutional amendment. While not endorsing specific language, Attorney

General Janet Reno testifies in support of federal constitutional rights for crime victims.

In June, the President reaffirms his support of federal constitutional rights for crime victims in a Rose Garden ceremony attended by members of Congress, criminal justice officials, and local, state, and national victims' rights organizations. Also that month, the Judiciary Committee in the U.S. House of Representatives conducts its first hearing on the proposed amendment.

In July the Crime Victims Assistance Act is introduced into the U.S. Senate, offering full-scale reform of federal rules and federal law to establish stronger rights and protections for victims of federal crime. This legislation further proposes to assist victims of state crime through the infusion of additional resources to make the criminal justice system more supportive of crime victims.

To fully recognize the sovereignty of Indian nations, OVC for the first time provides victim assistance grants in Indian country directly to the tribes.

A federal antistalking law is enacted by Congress.

1998

The Child Protection and Sexual Predator Punishment Act of 1998 is enacted, providing for numerous sentencing enhancements and other initiatives addressing sex crimes against children, including crimes facilitated by the use of interstate facilities and the Internet.

The Crime Victims with Disabilities Act of 1998 is passed, representing the first effort to systematically gather information on the extent of the problem of victimization of individuals with disabilities.

The Identity Theft and Deterrence Act of 1998 is signed into law in October 1998. This landmark federal legislation outlaws identity theft and directs the U.S. Sentencing Commission to consider various factors in determining penalties, including the number of victims and the value of the loss by any individual victim.

1999

On January 19, 1999, the Federal Victims' Rights Constitutional Amendment (Senate Joint Resolution 3, identical to SJR 44) is introduced before the 106th Congress.

The National Crime Victim Bar Association is formed by the National Center for Victims of Crime to promote civil justice for victims of crime.

2000

The Internet Fraud Complaint Center Web site (www.ifccfbi.gov) is created by the U.S. Department of Justice, Federal Bureau of Investigation, and the National White Collar Crime Center to combat Internet fraud by giving consumers nationwide a convenient way to report violations, and by centralizing information about fraud for law enforcement.

The U.S. Congress passes a new national drunk driving
limit of 0.08 blood alcohol concentration (BAC) with
the strong support of Mothers Against Drunk Driving and other victim advocacy organizations, as well
as leading highway safety, health, medical, law enforcement, and insurance groups.

In April 2000, the Federal Victims' Rights Constitutional Amendment (SJR 3) is addressed for the first
time by the full U.S. Senate. On April 27, 2000, following two and a half days of debate, SJR 3 is withdrawn for further consideration by its cosponsors,
Senators Kyl (R-AZ) and Feinstein (D-CA), when it
becomes apparent that the measure would not receive
a two-thirds majority vote necessary for approval.

2001

There were 3,047 victims of the terrorist attacks on
American soil on September 11, 2001: 2,175 males
and 648 females died at the World Trade Center; 108
males and 71 females died at the Pentagon; 20 males
and 20 females died in the plane crash in Somerset
County, Pennsylvania; and countless others were injured by these terrorist attacks.

Congress responds to the terrorism acts of September 11
with a raft of legislation, providing funding for victim assistance, tax relief for victims, and other accom-
modations and protections for victims. A new federal
compensation program specifically for the victims of

September 11 was created as a part of the Air Transportation Safety and System Stabilization Act.

As a part of the package of antiterrorism legislation called the USA Patriot Act of 2001, changes are made to the Victims of Crime Act (VOCA), including increasing the percentage of state compensation payments reimbursable by the federal government, and allowing OVC to fund compliance and evaluation projects.

2002

All fifty states, the District of Columbia, the U.S. Virgin Islands, Puerto Rico, and Guam have established crime victim compensation programs.

This list is based on information provided by the Office for Victims of Crime, National Crime Victims' Rights Week Resource Guide.

Getting Help: Resources and Strategies

DOMESTIC VIOLENCE

- *If you need immediate assistance, dial 911.*
- The National Domestic Violence Hotline: 800-799-7233.

Advice from the National Coalition
Against Domestic Violence:

If you are still in the relationship:

1. Think of a safe place to go if an argument occurs—avoid rooms with no exits (bathroom), or rooms with weapons (kitchen).
2. Think about and make a list of safe people to contact.

3. Keep change with you at all times.

4. Memorize all important numbers.

5. Establish a "code word" or "sign" so that family, friends, teachers, or coworkers know when to call for help.

6. Think about what you will say to your partner if he/she becomes violent.

7. Remember you have the right to live without fear and violence.

If you have left the relationship:

1. Change your phone number.

2. Screen calls.

3. Save and document all contacts, messages, injuries, or other incidents involving the batterer.

4. Change locks if the batterer has a key.

5. Avoid staying alone.

6. Plan how to get away if confronted by an abusive partner.

7. If you have to meet your partner, do it in a public place.

8. Vary your routine.

9. Notify school and work contacts.

10. Call a shelter for battered women.

If you leave the relationship, or are thinking of leaving, you should take important papers and documents with you to enable you to apply for benefits or take legal action. Important papers you should take include Social

Security cards and birth certificates for you and your children, your marriage license, leases or deeds in your name or both your and your partner's names, your checkbook, your charge cards, bank statements and charge account statements, insurance policies, proof of income for you and your spouse (pay stubs or W-2s), and any documentation of past incidents of abuse (photos, police reports, medical records, etc.)

CHILD ABUSE
National Child Abuse Hotline

800-4-A-CHILD

National Clearinghouse on Child Abuse and Neglect Information

330 C Street, SW
Washington, D.C. 20447
800-394-3366 or 703-385-7565
http://nccanch.acf.hhs.gov

Prevent Child Abuse America National Office

200 S. Michigan Avenue, 17th floor
Chicago, IL 60604
312-663-3520
www.preventchildabuse.org

KlaasKids Foundation

P.O. Box 925
Sausalito, CA 94966
415-331-6867
www.klaaskids.org

Reporting Child Abuse: Advice from the National Child Abuse Hotline

If you suspect abuse, reporting it can protect the child and get help for the family. Each state identifies mandatory reporters (groups of people who are required to report suspicions of child abuse or neglect). However, any concerned person can and should report suspected child abuse.

If you suspect a child is being harmed, contact your local child protective services (CPS) or law enforcement agency so professionals can assess the situation. When calling to report child abuse, you will be asked for specific information, which may include:

- The child's name.
- The suspected perpetrator's name (if known).
- A description of what you have seen or heard.
- The names of any other people having knowledge of the abuse.
- Your name and phone number.

Remember, your suspicion of child abuse or neglect is enough to make a report. You are not required to provide proof. Almost every state has a law to protect people who make good-faith reports of child abuse from prosecution and/or liability.

Your report of possible child maltreatment will first be screened by hotline staff or a CPS worker. If the worker feels there is enough credible information to indicate that maltreatment may have occurred, or is at risk of occurring, your report will be referred to staff who will conduct an investigation. In some states, reports of lower-risk situations are assigned to another agency or staff member, who will conduct an assessment of the family's needs.

Investigators respond within a particular time period (anywhere from a few hours to a few days), depending on the potential severity of the situation. They may speak with the child, the parents, and other people in contact with the child (such as doctors, teachers, or childcare providers). Their purpose is to determine if abuse or neglect has occurred, and if it may happen again.

If the investigator finds that no abuse or neglect occurred, or what happened does not meet your state's definition of abuse or neglect, the case will be closed and the family may or may not be referred elsewhere for services. If the investigator feels the children are at risk of harm, the family may be referred to services to reduce the risk of future maltreatment. These may include mental health care, medical care, parenting skills classes, employment assistance, and concrete support, such as financial or housing assistance. In rare cases where the child's safety cannot be ensured, the child may be removed from the home.

CHILD SEXUAL ABUSE
Stop It Now!

P.O. Box 495
Haydenville, MA 01039
413-268-3096, 888-PREVENT
www.stopitnow.com

**Behavioral Warning Signs That a Child
May Have Been Abused**

Some of these behavioral signs can show up at other stressful times in a child's life, such as divorce, the death of a family member, friend, or pet, or when there are problems in school—as well as when abuse is involved. Any one sign doesn't mean the child was abused; but several of them mean that you should begin asking questions. Do you notice some of the following behaviors in children you know well?

• Nightmares, trouble sleeping, fear of the dark, or other sleeping problems.
• Extreme fear of "monsters."
• Loss of appetite, or trouble eating or swallowing.
• Sudden mood swings such as rage, fear, anger, or withdrawal.

- Fear of certain people or places (e.g., a child may not want to be left alone with a baby-sitter, a friend, a relative, or some other child or adult; or a child who is usually talkative and cheery may become quiet and distant when around a certain person).
- Stomach illness all of the time with no identifiable reason.
- An older child behaving like a younger child, such as bed-wetting or thumb sucking.
- Sexual activities with toys or other children, such as simulating sex with dolls or asking other children/siblings to behave sexually.
- New words for private body parts.
- Refusing to talk about a "secret" he/she has with an adult or older child.
- Talking about a new older friend.
- Suddenly having money.
- Cutting or burning herself or himself as an adolescent.

Physical Warning Signs That a Child May Have Been Abused

Does a child close to you have the following:

- Unexplained bruises, redness, or bleeding of the genitals, anus, or mouth.
- Pain at the genitals, anus, or mouth.
- Genital sores or milky fluids in the genital area.

If you said yes to any of these examples, bring your child to a doctor. Your doctor can help you understand what may be happening and test for sexually transmitted diseases.

Keep Young Children Safe

Here are a few simple **do's** and **don'ts** to teach your children.

- **Don't** talk to strangers.
- **Don't** ever get into a car with a stranger.

You **don't** have to be afraid of people you don't know, but you **do** have to be careful.

If you are out in public and a stranger takes your hand:

- **Do** yell "He is *not* my dad" or "She is *not* my mom."

When you're with your parents:

- **Don't** wander off by yourself.
- **Do** stay with your parents.

If you are home alone, *follow these rules:*

- When you answer the phone, **do** tell the caller that your mom or dad is busy and take a message. **Don't** tell the caller you are at home by yourself!

- If the stranger calls again, **do** call the emergency number your parents gave you!
- If someone knocks on the door, **do** look through the peephole first to see who it is.
- If you **don't** know the person, **don't** answer.
- If the person keeps knocking, **do** use the emergency number your parents gave you or call a neighbor you trust.

Just to be extra *safe:*

- **Don't** go somewhere with *anyone,* even if you know the person, unless your parents have told you it is okay to do so.
- **Do** call your parents before you go anywhere with an adult.

In the event your child becomes lost or missing, contact your local police department **immediately.** Response time is of critical importance. For more information call:

National Center for Missing and Exploited Children

Charles B. Wang International Children's Building
699 Prince Street
Alexandria, VA 22314
703-274-3900
Hotline: 1-800-THE-LOST (843-5678)
www.missingkids.com

UNDERAGE DRINKING AND SUBSTANCE ABUSE
Prevention Decision Support System (PDSS)

What parents should do to protect their children from alcohol and drugs:

1. **Establish and maintain good communication with your children.**

   Talk with your children about alcohol, tobacco, and illegal drugs. Let them know that no topic is off-limits. Listen to them when they describe the pressures and problems they are encountering. Start the dialogue early. Children begin experimenting with alcohol and drugs as early as their preteen years. Teach your children the health, safety, and legal consequences of using alcohol, tobacco, or illegal drugs. Be open and communicate honestly. You might be surprised by just how much influence you have on your children's choices.

2. **Make clear rules and enforce them with consistency and appropriate consequences.**

   Let your children know what you expect of them. Be firm and consistent. A parent's role is as a guide and leader, not a friend. Make sure your children know that smoking, drinking alcohol, and using drugs will not be tolerated, and that there will be severe consequences if they engage in these behaviors.

3. Set an example for your children.

Be a positive role model. Children have a very sharp radar for parents whose message seems to be "Do what I say, not what I do." Also, through all ages of development, children tend to emulate their parents. Strive to keep yourself and all family members free from substance abuse. The more members of your family that set a positive example, the less likely your children will fall victim to substance abuse.

4. Monitor your children's activities.

Ask questions about what your children are doing, with whom, for how long, and where. Get to know the friends they spend time with and other parents as well. Be sure your children have easy access to a wide range of appealing, drug-free, alternative activities and safe, monitored areas where they can gather, especially after school.

Warning Signs and Symptoms of Substance Abuse

- Drop in school attendance or academic performance
- Isolation, depression, fatigue
- Increase in borrowing money
- Petty theft, especially of cash in small quantities
- Change in friends
- Uncharacteristic withdrawal from family, friends, or interests
- Physical changes (e.g., persistent runny nose, red eyes, coughing, wheezing, bruises, needle marks)

- Smell of alcohol on breath or sudden, frequent use of breath mints
- Missing or watered-down alcohol in liquor bottles in your liquor cabinet
- Sudden use of strong perfume or cologne
- Heightened secrecy about actions or possessions
- Use of incense or room deodorant
- Drug paraphernalia (e.g., rolling papers, eyedrops, lighters, pipes, cigars)

This on-line interactive tool developed by the Center for Substance Abuse Prevention (CSAP) is a step-by-step guide for those interested in developing community and statewide prevention programs. It covers procedures for doing needs assessments, building capacity, selecting the best and most promising interventions, and conducting evaluations. For more information see www.preventiondss.org/

Mothers Against Drunk Driving (MADD)

This grassroots organization, with more than 600 chapters nationwide, seeks effective solutions to drunk driving and underage drinking problems. To find the MADD chapter nearest you, see www.madd.org/chapters/

Community Anti-Drug Coalitions of America (CADCA)

CADCA is an organization that provides resources and training to community coalitions. For information on advocacy and coalition building, see http://cadca.org

National Institute on Alcohol Abuse and Alcoholism, NIH, DHHS

www.niaaa.nih.gov and www.alcoholfreechildren.org

Practical Suggestions

Leadership to Keep Children Alcohol Free, a program sponsored by the National Institute on Alcohol Abuse and Alcoholism, part of the National Institutes of Health in the U.S. Department of Health and Human Services, makes these suggestions as first steps in the campaign to prevent alcohol use by children in your community.

· Talk to your children about the dangers of early alcohol use. Encourage friends and neighbors to talk to their children.
· Ask your doctor or pediatrician to discuss alcohol use during your children's annual physicals.
· Support recreational alternatives to drinking and provide alcohol-free parties for young people.

- Encourage parents to learn about their responsibilities regarding alcohol access and service to children and adolescents in their homes.
- Talk to teachers, counselors, school administrators, and school board members to make sure that school prevention programs put equal emphasis on alcohol and illicit drug use.
- Place the issue of alcohol use by children on agendas for meetings of PTAs, the city council, faith groups, the Rotary Club, and other community groups and organizations.
- Start public discussions about alcohol use by the children in your community, with a focus on the messages your community is sending.
- Involve young people in your community's existing prevention efforts.
- Write letters to the editors of your local newspapers. Ask them to print articles about the dangers of early alcohol use.
- Personally contact elected and appointed officials at local and state levels to inform them about the problem and what can be done to solve it.
- Enlist increased support for immediate and consistent enforcement of existing underage alcohol-related drinking laws in your community.

National Highway Traffic Safety Administration, DOT: "2000 Youth Fatal Crash and Alcohol Facts"

This report documents actions that must be taken to reduce teenage alcohol-related fatalities. They include reaching the parents who ignore drinking by their underage children, increasing enforcement of laws shown to be effective in reducing fatalities, getting treatment for those hard-to-reach young people who are alcoholics or have drinking problems, and convincing young people that underage drinking, in addition to drinking and driving, is socially unacceptable. (www.nhtsa. dot.gov/people/injury/alcohol/Archive/2002YFCAF/ index.html)

Office of Juvenile Justice and Delinquency Prevention, OJP, DOJ
Strategies to Reduce Underage Alcohol Use: Typology and Brief Overview

This document provides a conceptual framework for understanding the array of strategies available to prevent underage alcohol use. It also provides a simple assessment of the level of effect that might be expected from each strategy, based on existing research and evaluation. (www.udetc.org/documents/strategies.pdf)

Regulatory Strategies for Preventing Youth Access to Alcohol: Best Practices

This document provides guidance on the best practices for shaping and implementing laws and regulations to restrict the commercial and social availability of alcohol to youth, and to deter young people from attempting to purchase or consume alcohol. (www.udetc.org/documents/accesslaws.pdf)

Substance Abuse and Mental Health Services Administration, DHHS
Prevention Enhancement Protocols System (PEPS)— Preventing Problems Related to Alcohol Availability: Environmental Approaches

This CSAP document, presented in three formats for three different audiences, provides an extensive discussion of the many approaches that communities can take to prevent alcohol use by underage youth. Suggested for broad use, the guidelines offer practical, detailed interventions, along with discussions of the advantages and disadvantages of these interventions. Each format is available on-line.

www.health.org/govpubs/PHD822/aap.htm
     (Practitioner Guide)
www.health.org/govpubs/PHD822/aar.htm
     (Reference Guide)

www.health.org/govpubs/PHD822/acc.htm
(Parent and Community Guide)

OTHER RESOURCES
**SAMHSA's National Clearinghouse for Alcohol
and Drug Information**

Substance Abuse and Mental Health Services
   Administration
Parklawn Building, room 12-105
5600 Fishers Lane
Rockville, MD 20857
800-729-6686
www.samhsa.gov

Tobacco Information and Prevention Source at CDC

www.cdc.gov/tobacco

Office of National Drug Control Policy

Drug Policy and Information Clearinghouse
P.O. Box 6000
Rockville, MD 20849
800-666-3332
www.whitehousedrugpolicy.gov

ONDCP's Youth Anti-Drug Campaign

www.theantidrug.com

Office of Juvenile Justice and Delinquency Prevention
Center for Substance Abuse Prevention's Strengthening
America's Families

www.strengtheningfamilies.org

**Children, Youth, and Families Education
and Research Network**

612-626-1111
www.cyfernet.org

ELDER ABUSE
National Center on Elder Abuse

1225 15th Street, NW, Suite 350
Washington, D.C. 20005
202-898-2586
www.elderabusecenter.org/

Older people and their families worry about crime, and
with good reason. Though the elderly are less likely to
be victims of crime than teenagers and young adults, the
number of crimes against older people is hard to ignore.
Each year about two million older people become crime
victims.

The elderly are targets for robbery, personal and car
theft, and burglary. Older people are more likely than
younger victims to face attackers who are strangers. They

are more often attacked at or near their homes. Chances are that an older victim may be more seriously hurt than a younger person.

It isn't only strangers who hurt older people. Sometimes family members, friends, or caretakers may physically, mentally, or financially abuse older people through neglect, violence, or by stealing money or property.

Even though there are risks, do not let a fear of crime stop you from enjoying life. There are things you can do to be safer. Be careful and be aware of what goes on around you.

Safety Tips for Seniors

You can fight crime. The best thing you can do at **home** is to lock your doors and windows. You can also protect yourself at home in other ways:

- Always try to see who's there *before* opening your door. Look through a peephole or a safe window. Ask any stranger to tell you his or her name and to show proof that he or she is from the identified company or group. Remember, it is okay to keep the door locked if you are uneasy.
- Make sure that locks, doors, and windows are strong and cannot be broken easily. A good alarm system can help. Many police departments will send an officer to your home to suggest changes that could improve your security.

- Mark valuable property by engraving an identification number on it, such as your driver's license number. Make a list of expensive items, such as jewelry or silver. Take a picture of the valuable items and store the details in a safe place, like a bank safety deposit box.
- Purchase an air horn and use it only in case of an emergency to frighten away intruders and signal your neighbors that something is wrong. Keep the air horn near the front door.

On the **street,** stay alert at all times, even in your own neighborhood and at your own door. Walk with a friend. Try to stay away from places where crimes happen, such as dark parking lots or alleys. You can also:

- Have monthly pension or Social Security checks sent direct-deposit, right to the bank. If you visit the bank often, vary the time of day you go.
- Don't carry a lot of cash. Try not to carry a purse. Put your money, credit cards, or wallet in an inside pocket. If you are stopped by a robber, hand over any cash you have.
- Don't dress in a flashy way. Leave good jewelry, furs, and other valuables in a safe place to avoid tempting would-be robbers.

Money and property crimes come in many forms and are a big problem. Older people may be victims of consumer fraud, such as con games or insurance scams. Even family members or friends can sometimes steal an older person's money or property. Trust what you feel. Protect yourself:

- Don't take money from your bank account if a stranger tells you to. In one common scam, a thief may pretend to be a bank employee and ask you to take out money to "test" a bank teller. Banks do not check out their employees this way.
- Stay away from deals that are "too good to be true." Beware of deals that ask for a lot of money up front and promise you sure success. Check with your local Better Business Bureau.
- Don't give your credit card or bank account number over the phone to people who have called you to sell a product or ask for a contribution.
- Don't be taken in by quick fixes or miracle cures for health problems. People who are not trained or licensed may try to sell you miracle "cures" for cancer, baldness, arthritis, or other problems. Ask your doctor before you buy. Be sure to go to licensed professionals.

Warning Signs of Elder Abuse

Physical

- Bruises in various stages of healing, which may appear as finger marks on the skin.
- Broken bones.

- Significant hygiene changes (soiled clothing, dirty hair, body/urine/feces odor, dirty/broken/long fingernails).
- Poor nutrition and hydration.
- Failure to take medication(s), which may result in gradual or sudden changes in affect and/or behavior. Dizziness and increased confusion may be signs.
- Sleeplessness and/or exhaustion.
- Sexual abuse may present as bruising, bloodstained and/or soiled undergarments, pain/bleeding/discharge in the genital area, or gait change due to pain and fear of the perpetrator.

Emotional

- Fearful of caregiver (e.g., flinching).
- Defensive behavior that is overprotective of the caregiver.
- Weepiness.
- Expressions of hopelessness.
- Increased confusion or signs of dementia.
- Depression.
- Isolation or withdrawal from social interaction and routines (friends, neighbors, relatives, synagogue/church).
- Agitation or hyperactivity—pacing, shuffling papers/clothing.

Financial

- Frequent cash withdrawals, especially when cash cannot be accounted for.

- Unpaid bills and/or collection notices.
- Utilities turned off.
- Increased and frequent credit card use.
- Inability to manage finances (makes older person a target).
- Denial of necessary services, such as home care by caregiver, for his or her own financial gain.
- Frequent "gift" giving (cash/checks).
- Evidence of being the victim of a mail or telephone scam—mail solicitations, large amounts of money unaccounted for, secretive behavior.

Identity Theft

- Large credit card bills with no proof of purchases.
- Sudden loss of real estate; notices that mortgage/taxes aren't being paid.
- Sudden increase in telephone bill, with calls listed that cannot be accounted for.

Environmental

- Empty refrigerator.
- Dirty and overcluttered apartment or home.
- Stacks of dirty dishes in the sink.
- Evidence of vermin—mice, rats, roaches.
- Odor of urine or feces, and stained furniture and/or clothing.
- Utilities shut off.
- Stacks of Meals-On-Wheels trays.

- Unopened mail/bills.
- Clothing strewn about the house.

In cases where a senior may be in imminent danger, it is essential that authorities are notified immediately. It is far better to err on the side of caution than to send a senior back to a dangerous situation. In the event of an emergency or imminent danger, please call 911.

Neglect or mistreatment of older people is called elder abuse. It can happen anywhere, at home by family or friends, or in a nursing home by other caregivers. Physical, financial, or emotional abuse by family or friends is very hard to deal with. There is help for people who are being abused. Most states and many local governments have adult protective services programs. Check the phone book or call directory assistance. You can also talk to your clergy, a lawyer, or a doctor. Your local area agency on aging may help. The Eldercare Locator (800-677-1116 or www.eldercare.gov/Eldercare/Public/Home.asp) can direct you to a local agency.

Reporting Crime

You can help your friends and neighbors by reporting crime when it happens. Police say that more than half of all crimes go unreported. If you don't report a crime because of embarrassment or fear, the criminals stay on the streets.

If you are the victim of a crime, there is help. Contact the National Organization for Victim Assistance (NOVA), 1750 Park Road, NW, Washington, D.C. 20010. NOVA's 24-hour hotline is 800-TRY-NOVA. Their Web site address is www.try-nova.org

OTHER RESOURCES
American Association of Retired Persons (AARP)

Criminal Justice Services
601 E Street, NW
Washington, D.C. 20049
202-434-2222
www.aarp.org

Council of Better Business Bureaus

4200 Wilson Boulevard, Suite 800
Arlington, VA 22203
703-276-0100
www.bbb.org

Ask for the pamphlet called "Tips on Elderly Consumer Problems," and other publications.

National Council on the Aging

300 D Street, SW, Suite 301
Washington, D.C. 20024
202-479-1200
www.ncoa.org

Publications are available on a variety of health-related consumer issues. Contact for a list of free publications.

ANIMAL ABUSE

Quick Facts:

- Animal abuse is a crime in every state; in 34 states it is a felony. It is a crime in every state to torture, abandon, or injure an animal; to fight an animal for sport or money; or to deprive an animal of food, water, shelter, or care.
- Animal abuse is linked to other forms of violence. Clinical studies indicate that for many violent offenders, their first victims were animals. For example, cruelty to animals was prevalent in the juvenile histories of serial killers such as Jeffery Dahmer, Ted Bundy, and David Berkowitz.
- Cruelty to animals has been linked to domestic violence. One study found that 85 percent of women and 63 percent of children entering domestic violence shelters reported that cruelty to animals had occurred in their homes.

- Illegal animal fighting promotes other forms of crime. Dog fighting in particular is linked to many other criminal activities, including gambling, gang membership, sale and possession of drugs, and possession of illegal weapons. Individuals who house dogs in abandoned buildings or garages are likely to be involved in dog fighting. The dogs often wear wide leather collars with heavy rings and studs, or have scars on the head, throat, legs, or ears, or may even be bleeding.

The American Society for the Prevention of Cruelty to Animals

424 East 92nd Street
New York, NY 10128
212-876-7700
www.aspca.org

Animal Cruelty/Law Enforcement

The ASPCA's Humane Law Enforcement agents inspect, rescue, and, when warranted, make arrests to protect animals within New York State. ASPCA agents conduct investigations based on calls from the public or other humane organizations about incidents of animal cruelty, neglect, or abandonment. The uniformed and plainclothes men and women investigate more than 5,000 cases per year and issue summonses to or arrest more than 300 people per year.

Animal Poison Control Center

The ASPCA Animal Poison Control Center is the only animal poison control center in North America. Established in 1978, the Center is the only facility of its kind, staffed by twenty-five veterinarians, including five board-certified veterinary toxicologists and ten certified veterinary technicians. Located in Urbana, Illinois, the specially trained staff provides assistance to pet owners and specific analysis and treatment recommendations to veterinarians pertaining to toxic chemicals and dangerous plants, products, or substances 24 hours a day, 7 days a week. In 2001, the Center handled over 65,000 cases. The Center also provides extensive veterinary toxicology expert consulting on a wide array of subjects that includes legal cases, formulation issues, product liability, and regulatory reporting. To reach The ASPCA Animal Poison Control Center you can call 888-426-4435. For more information on The ASPCA Animal Poison Control Center visit www.apcc.org

HATE CRIMES
Leadership Conference on Civil Rights

1629 K Street NW, 10th floor
Washington, D.C. 20006
202-466-3311
www.civilrights.org

Southern Poverty Law Center

400 Washington Avenue
    Montgomery, AL 36104
334-956-8200
www.splcenter.org

Simon Wiesenthal Center

1399 South Roxbury Drive
Los Angeles, CA 90035
310-553-9036
800-900-9036 (toll-free from within the U.S.)
www.wiesenthal.com

National Gay and Lesbian Task Force

1325 Massachusetts Ave. NW, Suite 600
Washington, D.C. 20005
202-393-5177
www.thetaskforce.org

Department of Justice, Victim Assistance Center

Terrorism victim hotline:

800-331-0075

800-833-6885 (TTY)

International callers: 00-1-414-359-9751 (call collect)

9 A.M.–5 P.M. EST Monday–Friday (GMT-5)

Translation services available

810 7th Street, NW

Washington, D.C. 20531

www.ojp.usdoj.gov/ovc/

www.ojp.usdoj.gov/ovc/familycallcenter.htm

IDENTITY THEFT

Identity theft is the fastest-growing crime in our country today. Last year alone, more than 9.9 million Americans were victims of identity theft, at a cost of roughly five billion dollars. Identity theft is financially and emotionally devastating to its victims. The identity thief can inflict substantial damage on the victim's assets, credit, and reputation without the victim's even being aware of it. The damage that the criminal causes in stealing another person's identity often takes far longer to correct than it took the criminal to commit the crimes.

The Do's and Don'ts of Identity Safety

Do's

- **Do** shred all credit cards, bank statements, and other financial papers before discarding them.
- **Do** review all bank, credit card, and phone records for accuracy.
- **Do** use secure Web sites for Internet purchases.
- **Do** be wary of anyone calling to "confirm" personal information.
- **Do** order a copy of your credit report from each of the three credit bureaus every year. (See contact information below.)
- **Do** remove your Social Security number from checks, driver's licenses, or other identification.
- **Do** deposit mail in U.S. Postal Service collection boxes.
- **Do** sign new credit cards immediately upon their receipt.

Don'ts

- **Don't** provide credit card information over the telephone.
- **Don't** discuss financial matters on wireless or cellular phones.
- **Don't** carry your Social Security card in your wallet.
- **Don't** leave mail in your mailbox overnight or on weekends.
- **Don't** put your credit card number or any other financial account number on the outside of an envelope.

- **Don't** lend your credit cards to anyone else.
- **Don't** leave receipts behind at ATM machines, bank counters, or gasoline pumps.

If You Become a Victim

Take immediate action. The time it takes you to respond to this type of theft can have serious consequences on your financial liability and the financial damage that the thief can do. Follow these simple steps to minimize the damage.

1. Contact the fraud department for each creditor, bank, or other service that provided the identity thief with unauthorized credit, goods, or services.
2. Report the identity theft to the major credit bureaus listed below. Follow up with a written request for a "Fraud Alert" notification to be placed in your credit file. Include a copy of one of your utility bills and a copy of your driver's license for this purpose.

> Equifax
> P.O. Box 740241
> Atlanta, GA 30374
> 800-685-1111
> www.equifax.com
>
> Experian
> 888-397-3742
> www.experian.com

TransUnion
P.O. Box 2000
Chester, PA 19022
800-888-4213
www.tuc.com

3. Contact your local police department to file a police report. Sending a copy of the police report to your creditors or financial institutions can speed up the process of absolving you of fraudulent debts and removing inaccurate information from your credit report.

For more information, contact the Federal Trade Commission's Identity Theft Hotline at 1-877-438-4338.

PROTECT YOUR CAR FROM THEFT

More than a million people a year are victims of auto theft. Don't think for a minute that your vehicle cannot be stolen. The truth is that no car is completely theft proof. Your goal should be to make your car a difficult target. Auto theft is primarily a crime of opportunity. Car thieves usually opt for the car that is easiest to steal. To illustrate this point, let's consider the following scenario:

There are two similar Honda Accords sitting in the parking lot of a restaurant. Both are locked, but one of them has an antitheft device (such as the Club) attached to the steering wheel. Which car do you think a thief would be more likely to steal? Although a professional thief knows ways to bypass the Club, he would nevertheless choose to steal the car without the additional security device simply because it's easier. Adding a visible antitheft device to your car is part of the "Layered Approach" recommended by the National Insurance Crime Bureau and endorsed by many law enforcement agencies. Let's look now at some layers of protection you can use to protect your car:

Layer 1: Common Sense

This one's simple and it doesn't cost you a thing.

- Lock your doors.
- Remove your keys from the ignition.
- Close your windows completely.
- Park in well-lit areas.

Layer 2: Visible or Audible Device

We all find vehicle alarms annoying when they go off. Even better, so do car thieves . . . and they tend to avoid autos with alarms or antitheft devices! Consider adding a visible or audible antitheft device to your vehicle:

- Audible alarm system
- Steering-wheel locks
- Steering-column collars

- Theft-deterrent decals
- Wheel locks
- Window etching

Layer 3: Vehicle Immobilizer

Thieves can bypass your ignition by hot-wiring a vehicle. But you can put the heat on the bad guys by installing or utilizing a vehicle immobilizer system:

- Smart keys with computer chips that must be present to start the vehicle
- Fuse cutoffs
- Kill switches
- Starter, ignition, and fuel disablers

Layer 4: Tracking System

The final layer is a tracking system that emits a signal to the police or a monitoring service when the vehicle is reported stolen. If your vehicle has a tracking system and is stolen, it can often be recovered faster and with less damage. Put your vehicle on the radar screen by installing a tracking device.

If your car has been stolen, please contact your local police department as soon as possible.

We gladly provide this compilation in the hope that it may prevent a tragedy. Help to build a better society. Don't be a victim.